CAMPAIGN

OF

THE INDUS

CAMPAIGN

OF

THE INDUS:

IN

A SERIES OF LETTERS FROM AN OFFICER OF THE BOMBAY DIVISION.

A. H. HOLDSWORTH, ESQ.

GYAN

Published by

Gyan Publishing House
5, Ansari Road
Daryaganj, New Delhi-110002
Phone: 011-47034999, 9811692060
E-mail: books@gyanbooks.com

Distribution Network
gyanbooks.com
India, USA, Canada, UK, Australia, France

ISBN: 978-81-212-9414-0 (PB)
First Published, 1840

2nd Impression 2023

Printed at: Gyan Press, Delhi.

CAMPAIGN OF THE INDUS
AUTHOR: A. H. HOLDSWORTH

CAMPAIGN

OF

THE INDUS.

CAMPAIGN

OF

THE INDUS:

IN

A SERIES OF LETTERS FROM AN OFFICER OF THE BOMBAY DIVISION.

WITH AN INTRODUCTION,

BY

A. H. HOLDSWORTH, ESQ.

1840.

INTRODUCTION.

THE circumstance of an English army penetrating into Central Asia, through countries which had not been traversed by European troops since Alexander the Great led his victorious army from the Hellespont to the Jaxartes and Indus, is so strong a feature in our military history, that I have determined, at the suggestion of my friends, to print those letters received from my son which detail any of the events of the campaign. As he was actively engaged with the Bombay division, his narrative may be relied upon so far as he had an opportunity of witnessing its operations; and it being my intention to have only a few copies printed, to give to those friends who may take an interest in his letters, I need not apologize for the familiar manner in which they are written, as they were intended by him only for his own family, without an idea of their being printed. A history, however, may be collected from them most honourable to the British soldiers, both Europeans and natives of India. They shew the patience with which, for more than twelve months, the soldiers bore all their deprivations and fatiguing marches through countries until then unknown to them, whether moving through arid sands or rocky passes, under a burning sun; or over desolate mountains, amidst the most severe frosts, with scarcely an interval of repose. Neither was their gallantry less conspicuous than their patience, when they had the good fortune to find an enemy who ventured to face them. Although the circumstances which his letters detail might well deserve a better historian than my son, yet are they of that high and honourable character, that they cannot lose any part of their value by his familiar manner of narrating them.

When I decided upon printing these letters, it became a matter of interest to place before the reader a short account of the countries in which the operations of the army were conducted, as well as of the native rulers who took part in, or were the cause of them; in order that the letters might be more clearly understood by those friends who have not felt sufficiently interested in the history of those countries to make any inquiries about them. But, before I do so, I shall draw the attention of the reader to the army of Alexander, to which I have before alluded.

Without entering into the causes which led to his extraordinary conquests, predicted by Daniel as the means ordained of God to overthrow the Persian empire, then under the government of Darius, certain it is that he conquered the whole of those countries which extend from the Hellespont to the Indus, when his career was arrested by his own soldiers. Having overrun Syria, Egypt, Media, and Parthia, keeping his course to the north-east, he not only passed the Oxus, and forced his way to the Jaxartes, but, pressed by the Scythians from its opposite shore, he crossed that river, and beat them in a decisive battle. From the Jaxartes he returned in a southern direction towards the Indus, and having suffered the greatest privations, and struggled with the most alarming difficulties during the time that he was engaged in the conquest of those mountainous districts, he at length reached Cabool, making himself master of Afghanistan. Here he appears to have halted for a considerable time, to refresh and re-equip his army, which, with the addition of 30,000 recruits, amounted to 120,000 men.

At this place, Alexander first came upon the scene

of the campaign referred to in the following letters. Here he meditated the invasion of India, intending to march to the mouth of the Ganges; but the conquest of that country was destined for a nation almost unknown in the days of Alexander, and lying far more remote from it than Greece; and, until the campaign of 1839 drew our armies to the western side of the Indus, the Sutlej was alike the boundary of Alexander's conquests to the east, as of those of England towards the west.

Alexander having prepared his army for this expedition, moved towards the Indus, taking many strong places on his march. Having crossed that river, the king of the country offered no resistance, but became the ally of Alexander, who expected to have found Porus, whose kingdom was on the other side of the Hydaspes, equally ready to submit. But it required the utmost skill of Alexander to cross the river, which he effected, and conquered Porus, after a most severe struggle, with the loss of his renowned charger, Bucephalus, and he was so pleased at the magnanimity of Porus that he not only gave him back his kingdom, but added several small states to it, making him a sincere ally. Alexander then continued his march towards the east, conquering all who opposed him, until he reached the banks of the Hyphasis (Sutlej), which he was about to cross, when his progress was arrested by murmurs and tumults in his camp. His soldiers declared their determination not to extend his conquests, and entreated him to return. He then marched back to the Acesines, gave the whole country as far as the Hyphasis to Porus, and thus made him ruler of the Punjab. Alexander encamped near the Acesines until the month of October, when the fleet which he built, consisting of 800 galleys and boats, being ready, he embarked his army and proceeded towards the Indus; but before he reached that river he came to two countries possessed by warriors who united their armies to oppose his progress. After beating them in many engagements, Alexander attacked the city of the Oxydracæ, into which the greater part of those armies had retired. Here his rash valour had nearly terminated his career: he was severely wounded in the side by an arrow, from the effects of which he was with difficulty restored to health. He then descended the river, a portion of his army marching on its banks, conquering every nation that opposed him. About the month of July he reached Patala (Tatta), where he built a citadel and formed a port for his shipping. He then proceeded, with part of his fleet, by the western branch of the river, to discover the ocean. This he accomplished at great hazard, when he sacrificed to the gods (particularly to Neptune), and besought them not to suffer any mortal after him to exceed the bounds of his expedition. He then returned to join the rest of his fleet and army at Patala, and to make arrangements for his march to Babylon. He appointed Nearchus admiral of his fleet, and having given him orders to ascend the Persian Gulf to the Euphrates, he commenced his march through Beloochistan, leaving Nearchus to follow him as soon as the season would permit. Alexander was more than sixty days in reaching the frontiers of Persia, during which time his army suffered such dreadful privations from want of food, that the soldiers were obliged to eat their own war-horses, and from the sickness consequent upon such a state of distress, his army was reduced to less than one-half of the number which left Patala. It is not necessary to follow him to Babylon, or to describe the voyage of Nearchus, who, having sailed up the Persian Gulf, united his forces to those of his royal master in the river Pasi-Tigris, near Susa. Enough, however, may be learned from this history to convince us that if such an army could be conducted 2000 years ago from the Hellespont to the Jaxartes and Indus, the march from the southern shores of the Caspian Sea to Cabool would require comparatively but very slight exertion, if those who have the means should have the desire also to accomplish it.

I can say little of my own knowledge of the political causes which gave rise to the war, as I am unacquainted with the affairs of India and the motives which actuated its governors; but a brief outline may be collected from a book lately published by the Hon. Capt. Osborne, military secretary to the Governor-General, to which I shall refer, after making some observations upon the countries through which the operations of the army were conducted, and particularly on the situation of Afghanistan, in reference to those persons who had before been, as well as those who were, its rulers, when Shah Shooja was restored by the British Government to its throne. These observations I have chiefly collected from the valuable work of that enterprising officer Lieut. Burnes, which he published after visiting those countries in 1831, 1832, and 1833.

The chief portion of the Bombay division of the army engaged in the operations to which these letters refer, landed at the Hujamree mouth of the Indus, and marching through Lower Sinde, by Tatta, ascended the Indus by its western bank. On arriving in Upper Sinde, it was found that Shah Shooja with his contingent, as well as the Bengal division of the army, had crossed the Indus *en route* from that Presidency, and had advanced towards Afghanistan, and that the Bombay division was to follow them. To effect this, the division marched through Cutch Gundava, and the Bolan Pass, which is situated in the mountains which divide the province of Sarawar, in Beloochistan, as well as Cutch Gundava, from Afghanistan. Having made their way through the Bolan Pass, the army entered the Shawl district of Afghanistan, and thence proceeded through the Ghwozhe Pass to Candahar, Ghuzni, and Cabool; at which last-mentioned place Shah Shooja's eldest son joined his father with some troops of Runjet Sing's, which had crossed the Indus from the Punjab, marching by Peshawur and the Kyber Pass. The division of the Bombay troops under General Willshire, having remained at Cabool about a month, returned to Ghuzni, and thence in a straight direction to Quettah, leaving Candahar some distance on the right; Capt. Outram, who commanded a body of native horse, preceding the main body of the division for the purpose of capturing the forts, or castles, belonging to those chiefs who had not submitted to Shah Shooja. From Quettah, General Willshire moved with a part of his division upon Kelat, and thence through the

Gundava Pass and Cutch Gundava to the Indus, where these troops were met by the rest of the division, which came from Quettah by the Bolan Pass. Hence they descended to Curachee to embark for their respective quarters in India. The fate of one of the regiments of the division, the 17th, as it is recorded in a Bombay paper, is most distressing. They embarked at Curachee for Bombay, and sailed in the morning with a fair wind and a fine breeze, but before the night closed in upon them the ship was fast aground upon a sandbank, off the Hujamree branch of the Indus, scarcely within sight of land. Everything was thrown overboard to lighten the ship, but in vain; she became a total wreck, and settled down to her main deck in the water. She fortunately, however, held together long enough to allow all the men to be taken on shore, which occupied three days, but with the loss of everything they had taken on board with them. The other regiments, we may hope, have been more fortunate, as they were not mentioned in the paper which gave this melancholy account of the 17th regiment.

Sinde, the country through which the army first passed, is divided into three districts, each governed by an Ameer, the chief of whom resides at Hydrabad, the second at Khyrpoor, and the other at Meerpoor;

and when Lieut. Burnes ascended the Indus, in 1831, the reigning Ameers were branches of the Beloochistan tribe of Talpoor. With these the chief of Kelat and Gundava, Mehrab Khan (who was related by marriage to the Ameer of Hydrabad), was more closely allied than any other prince: like them, he had been formerly tributary to Cabool, and had shaken off the yoke; and, possessing a very strong country between Afghanistan and Sinde, he became as useful as he had at all times proved himself a faithful ally to the Sindeans. Shikarpoor, with the fertile country around it, as well as Bukker, had formerly belonged to the Barukzye family of Afghanistan, and, although they still possessed Candahar, Cabool, and Peshawur, they had in vain endeavoured to withdraw Mehrab Khan from his alliance with the Sindeans, or to recover those lost possessions.

To understand the political state of Afghanistan, into which the army marched for the purpose of restoring Shah Shooja to its throne, it will be necessary to go back to the early part of the last century, when Nadir Shah had raised himself to the throne of Persia. His name having become formidable as a conqueror, he turned his thoughts to the conquest of India, and, assuming sufficient pretexts for breaking the relations of amity which he professed for the monarch of that country, he determined to invade it, and for that purpose began his march in 1738. Taking with him some of the chiefs of Afghanistan, he crossed the Punjab and entered Delhi. He there raised enormous contributions, and seized upon everything worth taking away; amongst other things the far-famed Peacock throne, in which was the renowned diamond called "The Mountain of Light." The spoils with which he returned to Persia were valued at nearly seventy millions of pounds sterling. It is not necessary to follow the history of Nadir; it will be enough to say that, amidst the confusion which followed his death, Ahmed Khan obtained possession of part of his treasure, amongst which was the great diamond. He escaped with it into Khorassan, where he made himself master also of a large sum of money which was coming to Nadir from India. Ahmed was a brave and intelligent man, had been an officer of rank under the Shah, and, being in possession of the treasure necessary for his purpose, he proclaimed himself king, and was crowned at Candahar "King of the Afghans." Ahmed was of the Suddoozye family, which were but a small tribe; but he was greatly assisted by the powerful Barukzye family, whose friendship he justly valued and made use of to his advantage: of this latter family Hajee Jamel was then the chief. Ahmed knew how to conciliate the independent spirit of his Afghan subjects, and by making frequent incursions on his neighbours, kept alive that spirit of enterprise which was congenial to their feelings; but from the time of his death the royal authority began to decline, as Timour, his son and successor, had neither the sense nor enterprise necessary to uphold it. Affairs became still worse under the sons of Timour. Shah Zumaun was of a cruel disposition, and wanted the education necessary to the situation he was called upon to fill; his brothers, Mahmood and Shah Shooja, were not better disposed; and towards the Barukzye family, who had been so instrumental in placing their grandfather, Ahmed, on the throne, they conducted themselves not only most imprudently, but with dreadful cruelty.

Shah Zumaun was succeeded by Shah Shooja, of whom, although the chief person in the present drama, little more need be said of this part of his history than that, ignorant of the mode of governing such independent tribes as the Afghans, his power was never great, and, after the fall of his vizier, and the murder of his comrade, Meer Waeez, it gradually declined, until he lost his throne at Neemla, in 1809. He had taken the field with a well-appointed army of 15,000 men; but was attacked by Futteh Khan, an experienced general, at the head of 2000 men, before the royal army was formed for battle; Akram Khan, his vizier, was slain, and he fled to the Kyber country, leaving the greater part of his treasure in the hands of his conquerors. Shah Shooja had failed to conciliate the Barukzye family; Futteh Khan, their chief, had therefore espoused the cause of the king's brother, Mahmood, and having driven Shah Shooja from his throne, he placed Mahmood upon it, and accepted for himself the situation of vizier. Under his vigorous administration, the whole of the Afghan country, with the exception of Cashmere, submitted to the dominion of the new sovereign. The Shah of Persia, anxious to possess himself of Herat, sent an army against it, but was defeated in his object, and Herat was preserved to Mahmood by the successful exertions of Futteh Khan. No sooner, however, was Mahmood thus firmly established in his dominions, than his son Kamran became jealous of the man who had raised him to the situation, and had secured to him the kingdom; he therefore determined to effect the ruin of the vizier. The prince was not long in gaining over his father to his views; and Futteh Khan being at Herat, Kamran seized on his person and put out his eyes. In this state he kept him prisoner for about six months, during which time the brothers of the vizier, irritated at the conduct of Kamran, began to show signs of disaffection. Mahmood ordered Futteh Khan to be brought before him in the court of his palace, and accusing the brothers of the vizier of rebellion, directed him to bring them back to a state of allegiance. The vizier, in the dreadful condition to which he had been reduced, replied to the demand of Mahmood, "What can an old and blind man do?" when, by the order of the king, the courtiers cut the vizier to pieces, limb after limb: his nose and ears were hacked off; neither did he receive his death blow until not a member of his person was left upon which they could inflict torture. With the fall of his vizier the king's power rapidly declined, and he fled to Herat, virtually yielding up the rest of his kingdom. He died in 1829, his son, Kamran, succeeding to the limited government of that portion only of his former dominions. Upon the flight of Mahmood to Herat, the horrid murder of their brother threw the whole of the Barukzye family into open revolt, the eldest of whom, Azeem Khan, recalled Shah Shooja from his exile. From the time Shah Shooja lost his throne, he had been first a captive in the hands of the son of his former vizier, and then a pensioner on the bounty of the Maharajah, at Lahore, who in return extorted from him the famous diamond, "The Mountain of Light," and other jewels, which he had brought away with him when he fled at Neemla. He then made his escape from the Maharajah, and found protection and support from the British government of India. Upon the summons from Azeem Khan, Shah Shooja immediately hastened to Peshawur; where, before his benefactor had time to meet him, he practically displayed his ideas of royalty so unwisely, and so insulted some of the friends of the Barukzye family, that the whole party took offence, and they at once rejected him, and placed his brother Eyoob on the throne.

Eyoob was but a puppet king, the tool of the family who raised him to the government; Azeem Khan, who was appointed his vizier, being in truth the ruler. Several of the young princes who aspired to the throne were delivered over to Eyoob, who put them to death.

Shooja, driven from Peshawur, retired to Shikarpoor, which the Ameers of Sinde ceded to him; where, in place of conducting himself with prudence, he was so addicted to low intrigue with those about him, that his enemies availed themselves of this propensity to effect his ruin, and drove him from Shikarpoor, when, crossing the Indus, he fled through the desert by Juydalmeer, and returned to Loodiana. "The fitness," says Lieut. Burnes, "of Shah Shooja-ool-Moolk for the station of a sovereign seems ever to have been doubtful. His manners and address are highly polished, but his judgment does not rise above mediocrity; had the case been otherwise, we should not now see him an exile from his country and his throne, without a hope of regaining them, after an absence of twenty years, and before he has attained the fiftieth year of his age."

The civil wars which had thus so frequently occurred in Afghanistan weakened the resources of the country and its means of defence. Runjet Sing availed himself of the advantage which this state of affairs presented to him, and obtained possession of Cashmere; when, continuing his conquests, he crossed the Indus, and made himself master of Peshawur, burning its palace, and laying the country under tribute. Azeem Khan made a precipitate retreat before the army of the Sikhs towards Cabool, without attempting to arrest their progress, and was so stung with remorse at the weakness of his conduct that he died on reaching that city. With the death of Azeem the royal authority was extinguished. The king fled to Lahore, and lived under the protection of his conqueror. Herat alone remained in the possession of one of the Suddoozye family. The brothers of the late vizier seized his son, and deprived him of his treasure and his power. The kingdom was then divided between them. Cabool fell into the hands of Dost Mahomed; Peshawur and Candahar were held by two of his brothers; the Sindeans threw off their yoke, and refused to pay tribute; Balk was annexed to the dominions of the King of Bokhara; the richest portion of the provinces having fallen into the possession of the Sikhs. In seventy-six years from the time that Ahmed Shah was crowned at Candahar, the Dooranee monarchy again ceased to exist.

As I have given the character of Shah Shooja, it will be interesting to quote that of Dost Mahomed, from the same author. "He is unremitting in his attention to business, and attends daily at the court-house, with the Cazee and Moollahs, to decide every cause according to law. Trade has received the greatest encouragement from him, and he has derived his own reward, since the receipts of the custom-house of the city have increased fifty thousand rupees, and furnished him with a net revenue of two lacs of rupees per annum. The merchant may travel without a guard or protection from one frontier to another, an unheard-of circumstance in the time of the kings. The justice of this chief affords a constant theme of praise to all classes. The peasant rejoices at the absence of tyranny, the citizen at the safety of his home, the merchant at the equity of his decisions and the protection of his property, and the soldier at the regular manner in which his arrears are discharged." "One is struck with the intelligence, knowledge, and curiosity which he displays, as well as at his accomplished manners and address."

To this short sketch of Afghanistan, and of the persons connected with its political history, I will add some extracts from the work of the Hon. Capt. Osborne, because they explain the circumstances which led to the campaign of the Indus, and to the restoration of Shah Shooja to the throne of Cabool. He says, "In May, 1838, a complimentary deputation was sent by Runjet Sing to the Governor-General at Simla, consisting of some of the most distinguished Sikh chiefs, who were received with all the honours prescribed by oriental etiquette. Shortly afterwards, Lord Auckland resolved to send a mission to the court of Lahore, not merely to reciprocate the compliments of the Maharajah, but to treat upon all the important interests which were involved in the existing state of political affairs in that quarter of the world. The recent attempts of the Persians on Herat, the ambiguous conduct of Dost Mahomed, and the suspicions which had been excited with respect to the proceedings and ulterior designs of Russia, rendered it of the greatest importance to cement the alliance with Runjet Sing, and engage him to a firm and effective co-operation with us in the establishment of general tranquillity, the resistance of foreign encroachment, and the extension of the benefits of commerce and the blessings of civilization. Accordingly, W. H. Macnaghten, Esq., was deputed on the mission to the Maharajah, accompanied by Dr. Drummond, Capt. Macgregor, and the Hon. W. Osborne, military secretary to the Governor-General.

"The object of the Governor-General's mission to Lahore having been accomplished, and the concurrence, and, if necessary, the co-operation of Runjet Sing, in the restoration of Shah Shooja, secured, Mr. Macnaghten repaired to Loodiana, for the purpose of submitting to the Shah the treaties that had been concluded, and announcing to him the approaching change in his fortunes. The envoys seem to have been much struck with the majestic appearance of the old pretender, especially with the flowing honours of a black beard descending to his waist, always the most cherished appendage of oriental dignity. He had lived for twenty years in undisturbed seclusion, if not 'the world forgetting,' certainly 'by the world forgot,' consoling himself for the loss of his kingdom in a domestic circle of six hundred wives, but always 'sighing his soul' towards the mountains and valleys of

Afghanistan, and patiently awaiting the *kismet*, or fate, which was to restore him to his throne. The preparations thenceforward went rapidly on. The contingent raised by the Shah was united (more for form than use) to the British force, and in three months the expedition began its operations."

But before I conclude this introduction to the letters, which detail the results of these treaties with the Maharajah, and the march of Shah Shooja to Cabool, as I have spoken of the leading characters of Afghanistan, I may be permitted to say a few words about the persons through whose exertions the Shah has been restored to the throne of that country—the officers of the British army; and I do so the more anxiously, because the naval and military glory of our country, which in my early days was the theme of every song, is now seldom heard of in society, and those gallant services appear to be nearly forgotten, which during a long protracted state of warfare, within our own recollection, placed England in a position to dictate her own terms of peace to the world:—a state of society which encourages a certain class of persons the more effectually to abuse the military profession, and to mislead their deluded followers, by clamouring about the expense of the army, and the aristocratic bearing of its members, that they may the more readily carry out their own schemes of personal vanity and demoralizing political economy.

It is the peculiar feature of the British army, to which we are indebted for its high and honourable bearing, that the sons of the first families in the land are ever anxious to bear arms under its standards, looking not to pecuniary emolument, but to those honours which military rank and professional attainments can procure for them; whilst the first commands and the highest stations in the service are filled without distinction from every grade in society. It is this happy mixture which induces that high sense of honour, so peculiarly characteristic of our service; that acknowledged distinction between the officers and the privates; that true discipline which, tempered with justice and kindly feeling, wins the respect of the soldier, and induces him to place that reliance upon his commander everywhere so conspicuous, whether in the camp or field of battle. But this high feeling in the army causes no additional expense to the country; the charge is altogether a deception. Let the following sketch of a young soldier's life of the present day, as applicable to others as to himself, answer the charge of these politicians.

He was educated for the highest walk of the legal

profession, and had nearly prepared himself for the university, when he decided to change his course and go into the army. The Commander-in-chief placed his name amongst the candidates for commissions, and he went to Hanover, where, after he had made himself master of the German language, his Royal Highness the Duke of Cambridge kindly gave him a commission in the Yagers of the Guard, better known in England, in the Peninsula, and at Waterloo, as the Rifles of the German Legion. Being only a volunteer in the regiment, he could not receive pay from the government; he was, therefore, at very considerable personal expense to keep his proper standing with his brother officers; and as soon as he had acquired all the military knowledge that he was likely to get in the regiment in time of peace, he obtained leave to return to England; and, as he had not any immediate expectation of a commission, he visited France, to make himself more perfect in the French language. After this, he was allowed to purchase a commission in the 2nd regiment, or Queen's Royals; and he embarked to join that corps in India. His letters will shew what that regiment, in common with others, have endured during a campaign of fifteen months in Central Asia, their privations and expenses; and when his second commission was paid for, during that campaign, he found himself at its close, at the age of twenty-five, a lieutenant on full pay, the amount of which, if he was in England, would be far short of the interest of the money which has been expended in his commissions and education, and with fifteen lieutenants still above him on the roll of his regiment.

It will be seen by his letters, and it is confirmed by the official despatches of the Commander-in-chief, that the company to which he was attached (the light company of the Queen's) led the storming party at Ghuzni. He was shot through the arm and through the body, and left for dead at the foot of the citadel at Kelat, whilst endeavouring to save the lives of some Beloochees who were crying for mercy. And for these services he is to be rewarded with a medal, by Shah Shooja, for Ghuzni, and for the capture of both places he has the full enjoyment of the highest gratification that a soldier can feel—the consciousness that he has done his duty to his country, and, let me hope, in the act of mercy in which he suffered, his duty to his God as a Christian. But he is not a solitary example of such good fortune. No one who was wounded and survived may have been nearer death than himself, yet are there others who have done more, and suffered more, as the history of the army of the Indus would bear ample testimony.

Let me then ask, in behalf of the British officer, when he is lightly spoken of as a man, or when the expenses of the army are cavilled at, on which side is the debt—on his, or on that of his country?

A. H. HOLDSWORTH.

Brookhill,—May, 1840.

☞ It may be right to draw the attention of the reader to a circumstance which, at first sight, may appear singular—that the same letters frequently contain reports quite contradictory to each other. It should therefore be borne in mind that such letters were probably written at different times, as the writer found opportunity; who, being anxious that his family should know all that passed as well in the camp as in the field, preferred leaving each report in the way in which it was circulated at the time of his writing it, rather than correct it afterwards, as the truth might turn out. Such letters shew the situation in which an army is placed on its landing in a new country, where no account of the movements of the inhabitants can be relied upon, and the heavy responsibility which attaches to the officers who are entrusted with its command.

CAMPAIGN OF THE INDUS.

LETTER I.

On board the ship Syden,
Off the mouth of the Indus, Nov. 27th, 1838.

My dear Father,—We left Belgaum on the 22nd of last month, and arrived at Bombay on the first of this; and we started from Bombay on the 18th, for this place. I had intended to write from Bombay, but everything was in such a state of confusion and bustle whilst we were there, that I literally could find no time or place for doing so. We are now at anchor off one of the mouths of the Indus, and have had a delightful voyage. Our ship is a very nice one, of 750 tons, belonging to a Swede, who is an excessively good fellow, and has treated us very well.

Sir John Keane is already arrived in the steamer Semiramis, and also one of the native regiments. Our Bombay force consists of 5500 men, of which 2000 are Europeans—viz., 500 of the Queen's, and 500 of

H. M. 17th regiment, one squadron of the 4th Light Dragoons, with foot and horse artillery. The rest of the force is composed of native regiments, horse and foot. We shall not land, I think, until to-morrow evening, as we are almost the only ship that has yet arrived. The infantry are divided into two brigades, and the cavalry form another by themselves. Our brigade (the first) consists of the Queen's, and the 5th and 19th regiments of Native Infantry, commanded by our worthy Colonel, now General Willshire, C.B.; the other brigade is commanded by a Company's officer. We have to go in boats about thirty miles, it is said, up the river, before we finally march. Where it is I am perfectly ignorant; however, some place between this and Hydrabad, whence we shall march as far north as Shikarpoor, where we are to form a junction with the Bengal troops, 13,000 in number, under Sir H. Fane. What our destination will be after that I know not; whether we shall advance with the Bengalees upon Herat, or form a corps of reserve on the Indus.

The country between this and Shikarpoor belongs to the Ameers of Sinde. They were very restive at first, when they heard of our intention to march through their country, and threatened to oppose our progress; but I believe they have since thought better of it; however, I do not think that they can do anything against us: time will soon shew. We have been excessively crowded on board: twenty-six officers.

I have been obliged to sleep on the poop every night, which, when the dew was heavy, was by no means pleasant. I hope we shall go further than Shikarpoor, as I should like very much to see Cabool, Candahar, and all that part of the world, which so few Europeans have visited.

What is the cause of all this bustle and war I hardly know myself, and, at all events, it is too long to make the subject of a letter; I must therefore refer you to the papers for it; but I have heard from old officers that for the last twenty years the Company have been anxious to establish themselves west and north of the Indus. It is not likely, therefore, now that they have such an opportunity, that they will let it slip, so that perhaps we may be quartered there for the next two or three years. How it will turn out I know no more than the man in the moon: a soldier is a mere machine, and is moved by his superiors just as a chessman by a chess-player. Should there be any skrimmaging, our men are in high spirits, and will, I think, soon make the Ameers put their pipes in their pockets. Ours is the first European army that has been on the Indus since the time of Alexander.

I was obliged to sell my horses and other things on leaving Belgaum, at a dead loss. I intend buying another horse when we land in Sinde, as I am told we can get good ones very cheap there. This is a regular case of here to-day and there to-morrow: perhaps my next letter may be dated from Cashmere—

who knows? I felt rather sorry at leaving Belgaum; we were all of us excessively rejoiced to get out of Bombay. The report at first was, that we were to garrison it for the next two or three years, and we were therefore very glad when we found that was not to be the case. Now, it is said, there is a chance of our going into Persia; but I do not think that we shall. The man waits to lay the cloth on the cuddy table, where I am writing, so I must conclude for the present.

Nov. 28th.—The regiment is beginning to disembark right in front. The Grenadiers are now going into the boats of the natives that are to take them up the river. Since I wrote yesterday, I have heard all the news relative to our disembarkation. We are to go fifteen miles up the river in native boats to a place called Vicur, where we form our first camp ground. We are to remain there for a week or ten days, in order to collect camels, bullocks, &c., for the transportation of our baggage. We have to pass a very dangerous bar in getting to this place, where several boats have been wrecked; but we have fine large ones. From all accounts, the Ameers are now peaceably disposed, except one fellow, who, we hear, is inclined to be rather obstreperous; but I think the sight of our force will soon bring him to his senses. There are, however, a set of men who live on the mountain borders of Sinde, called Beloochees, the eastern inhabitants of Beloochistan, who are a robber, free-and-easy kind of people, who may give us some trouble, in endeavouring to walk off with part of our baggage, &c.

I intend to keep a journal of what occurs, and will write by every opportunity. I think I have now mentioned everything that I have heard relative to this grand expedition; except, by-the-bye, that Sir Henry Fane has denominated the force as "The army of the Indus," and ours, the Bombay branch of it, as "The corps d'armée of Sinde." There is a grand title for you! I have nothing more to say; and as I must be looking after my traps previous to disembarking, I must conclude with best love to you, and all at home.

Your most affectionate son,

T. W. E. HOLDSWORTH.

P. S.—I must trust this to the captain of the vessel, giving him instructions to put it into the Bombay post when he returns, so that it is equally doubtful when you may receive it. He is an excessively good fellow, the captain; and we are going to make him a present of a silver goblet, worth 35*l.*, for his attentions to us whilst on board his ship.

LETTER II.

Perminacote, five miles from Vicur,
right bank of the Hujamree,
one of the branches of the Indus,
December 8th, 1838.

My dear Kitty,—I wrote to my father, about ten days ago, from the ship in which we came here, stating what I then knew about this expedition; but having since received your letter, and my father's, dated Sept. 4th, I cannot think of going on this bloody campaign without first answering yours. Things look now a little more warlike. The Ameers have endeavoured to cut off everything like a supply from this part of the country, and we have to depend in a great measure, at present, on the supplies brought by the shipping. We have nothing in the shape of conveyance for our baggage. We expected two thousand camels and five hundred horses here for sale; but they are not to be seen at present, and where they are, or when they will arrive, no one knows. News has been received, it is said, from Pottinger, the Company's political agent at Hydrabad, the principal town of the Ameers, that they have called in their army, consisting of 20,000 Beloochees, as they tell Pottinger, "for the purpose of paying them off;" but he says it looks very suspicious, and that they are also fortifying the various towns on the Indus. He has been expected here for the last two or three days, but has not yet arrived. Report also says that he has been fired at in his way down.

We are kept in the most strict discipline, and have a great deal to do. Out-lying and in-lying pickets every night, the same as if we were in the presence of an enemy. This is a very pleasant climate at present, though excessively cold at night-time, as we feel to our cost when on picket, sleeping in the open air, with nothing but our cloaks to cover us; and some nights the dew is excessively heavy, which is very unhealthy, and has laid me up for the last few days with an attack of rheumatism. However, I hope to be out of the sick list to-day. There is such a sharp, cutting, easterly wind, that I can hardly hold my pen. It averages from 80 to 84 in the shade during the hottest part of the day, but that is only for about two hours. However, in the hot season it is worse than India; and we have proof here, even at this time, of the power of the sun occasionally; so I hope that we shall push on for Shikarpoor, and join the Bengal army, under Sir H. Fane, as quickly as possible, as we shall then have some chance of getting to Cabool, which is said to be a delightful climate.

We are still totally ignorant of our future proceedings, except what I have stated above. We are in great hopes that we have not been brought here for nothing, and that we may have a chance of seeing a few hard blows given and taken ere long. Hydrabad and *lootè* is what is most talked about at present. It will, however, be a most harassing kind of warfare, I expect, as the force of the Ameers consists of Arabs and Beloochees; a regular predatory sort of boys, capital horsemen, but not able, I should think, to engage in a regular stand-up fight. I think their warfare will consist in trying to cut off a picket at night, breaking through the chain of sentries, and endeavouring to put the camp in confusion, &c. &c.; so that the poor subalterns on picket will have anything but a sinecure there; however, it will be a capital way of learning one's duty in the field. By-the-bye, I forgot to tell you, amongst other rumours of war, that an Ameer was down here a few days ago to obtain an interview with Sir J. Keane, who refused to see the Ameer, or to have anything to do with him, and told him that he would soon talk to him at Hydrabad.

Our force is now nearly all arrived, all except the Bombay grenadier regiment, which is to form part of ours, (i. e., the first brigade,) and not the 19th regiment, as I told my father. We have now here two squadrons of H. M. 4th Light Dragoons, the Queen's, and the 17th regiment. The native regiments are, the Grenadiers, the 5th, the 19th, and the 24th; there is also a due proportion of horse and foot artillery, together with some native cavalry, making in all 5500 fighting men. We are now about fifteen miles from the sea, and we got up quite safe, although there is a very dangerous bar to cross, and all the boats were not so lucky as ours, as the horse artillery lost fifteen horses; and a boat belonging to a merchant of Bombay went down, in which goods to the amount of one thousand rupees (100*l.*) were lost.

Our camp presents a very gay appearance—so many regiments collected together; and altogether I like this sort of campaigning work very well, although I expect that we shall be very hard put to it when we march, if we do not get more means of conveyance. The wind is blowing such intolerable dust into the tent that I can hardly write. The captain of the vessel which brought us from Bombay came up here last night, and returns to-day about eleven o'clock, and sails this evening for Bombay; I shall give him this letter to take, so that you and my father will receive my letters at the same time. As long as I keep my health I do not care where we go or what we do. The doctor has just come in and put me off the sick list. It is getting very near eleven o'clock, and the captain will be off directly, so that I must conclude my letter, hoping you will, for this reason, excuse its shortness; and with best love, &c., to all at home, believe me ever your most affectionate brother,

T. W. E. Holdsworth.

P.S. I have not any horse at present, which I find a great inconvenience. I sold what I had at Belgaum, before I left it, at a dead loss, as I expected to get plenty here on my arrival, but have been wofully disappointed. There were some splendid creatures for sale at Bombay, which was very tempting, but they asked enormous sums for them. I wonder where I shall eat my Christmas dinner! This is the first European army that has been on the Indus since the time of Alexander the Great.

LETTER III.

Camp near Tatta, four miles from the Indus,
January 1st, 1839.

MY DEAR FATHER,—I write to wish you a happy new year on this the first day of 1839, which, if it turns out as its opening prognosticates, is likely to be a very eventful one for me, if I do not get knocked on the head or otherwise disposed of. I wrote to you from the ship Syden, about the 28th of November, and to Kate from our last station at Bominacote, on the right bank of the Hujamree, about the 12th of last month, both which letters will, I expect, leave Bombay to-day by the overland mail for England; but as another mail will leave on the 19th, and I thought you would be anxious to learn as much of our movements &c. as possible, I dare say the present letter will not be amiss.

We remained at our old encampment, Bominacote, until the 26th of last month, and I picked up my health very fast there, and was able to enjoy myself shooting a great deal, particularly the black partridge, which is an uncommonly handsome bird, and much bigger than the English. The 2nd brigade of infantry, consisting of H. M. 17th regiment, the 19th and 23rd regiments Native Infantry, under the command of General Gordon, a Company's officer, together with the 4th Light Dragoons, a regiment of Native Cavalry, and one troop of horse artillery, left the aforesaid place on the 24th, with Sir John Keane and his escort; and the first brigade, consisting of ourselves, the 1st Grenadiers, and 5th regiment Native Infantry, under the command of our chief, General Willshire, left on the 26th. I was on out-lying picket the night before, (Christmas night,) and a very curious way it was of passing it. The first part of the night, till twelve o'clock, was exceedingly fine and beautiful, and, as I lay on the cold ground, my thoughts travelled towards poor old Devonshire, and I could not help fancying in what a much more comfortable way you must be spending it at home, all snug, &c. at Brookhill. After twelve, the strong northerly wind, which blows with great force at intervals this time of the year in this country, sprung up, and it soon got intensely cold. Towards two I forgot myself for about half an hour, and nodded on my post, and on awakening I was taken with what I am sure must have been a slight attack of cholera. I was stone cold, particularly my arms, hands, legs, and feet, and suffered excruciating pains in my stomach, till nature relieved me, which she was kind enough to do uncommonly frequent. I had luckily some brandy with me, of which I drank, I should think, half a bottle down without tasting it; but it did me a great deal of good at the time, although I have not been well since, and am still very far from being so. Our camels, of which I had two, were furnished us by the commissariat, and we ought to have had them at four o'clock on the day before; but, like everything else, we did not get them till four o'clock the morning we marched, about an hour before we turned out. I had to trust entirely to Providence with regard to mine, as to whether I should get them or not, as I was on outlying picket, and could not attend to them, and I had just two minutes, after coming from picket in the morning, to get a mouthful of villanous coffee, when I was obliged to fall in with my company, which formed the advanced guard of the brigade, and march off in double quick time, leaving all to chance. My poor stomach wanted something most awfully to stop its proceedings, but it was totally out of the question, as General Willshire hurried us off at a slapping pace; luckily, the march was only eight miles, so it did not fatigue me much: I marched on foot the whole of it, as I could not get my pony in the hurry of starting. We got nothing to eat till two o'clock, when part of our mess things arrived, and we pitched into whatever we could get. This march, though, was by far the most pleasant, as we had a good firm tract of country to pass over, and no sand. The "rouse" sounded at five, and we marched again at half-past six. This night I was on in-lying picket, and was obliged to pass it in harness, and ready to turn out at a moment's notice, although awfully tired. We had a very unpleasant march, as the north winds got up soon after we started, and blew the dust and sand right into our eyes; we had, however, being on the advance guard, comparatively easy work, as there were only two sections with each officer: the poor column suffered severely. This day, however, was paradise compared to the next, which was eighteen miles, through an uninhabited sandy desert, with a few tamarisk shrubs and no water, except a few stagnant pools, which was the cause of the march being so long, there being no place for encampment. General Willshire, however, made the best of a bad matter, and sent on the night before to a place about half way, and the least unchristian-like spot he could find, half the men's rations for the next day, together with the bheesties (or water carriers) and the men's grog, &c., with orders for the cooks to have these rations cooked and ready for the men as soon as they marched in; so that on arriving at the ground we piled arms and formed a curious sort of pic-nic in the middle of the desert. We halted here about an hour, and lucky it was that the men got the means of recruiting their strength in this manner, as the latter part of the march was a terrible teaser. We marched off from this place about twelve. Although we had found the morning pleasant enough, with a fine bracing breeze, yet in the afternoon, about half an hour after starting, the wind went down, and the sun shone out terribly; the sand in some parts was half knee deep, and although there was no breeze to blow it in our faces, yet it rose from the trampling of so many feet in successive dense columns, and completely enveloped the whole brigade, almost blinding the men, so that they could hardly see the man before them, and getting into their noses and mouths so as nearly to suffocate them; however, they bore it manfully, and marched straight through it like Britons. Our encampment that night was at a place called Golam Shah, on the Buggaur, one of the branch streams of the Indus. We found that the second brigade had only left it the same morning, having been obliged to halt there the preceding day; and General Willshire found a letter from Sir John Keane, advising a halt there for the following day, which we accordingly did, and a precious comfortable day we had. I got off my pony at the close of this day's march with a dreadful headache, and had to wait for an hour till Halket's tent and kit, with whom I am doubling up, arrived. His servants brought me the delightful intelligence that my camel man had bolted with his camels at our last encampment, and that my things were all left there on the ground, with my servant, and that it was quite uncertain when they would be up; in fact, it seemed exceedingly doubtful whether they would arrive at all.

However, they did come in at last, but very late, on three ponies, two bullocks, and one donkey, which were the only things my boy could get, and for which I had to pay considerably. I turned in as soon as I could; and the next day, which was a most wretched one, I was very unwell. This place, Golam Shah, must, I think, be one of the most wretched places in the whole world, situated as it is in the heart of a desert, with only one recommendation,—viz., the river Buggaur, the water of which is excessively sweet and wholesome. The day we passed at it was the coldest I remember since leaving England. A strong northerly wind blew the whole day, and the clouds of dust and sand that rose in consequence were so thick as perfectly to obscure the sun, and all we could do we could not keep ourselves warm. Here we had the misfortune also to lose the only man that has as yet fallen on the march, an old soldier. He was taken with cholera at eight in the morning and died at twelve at night: he was buried about six hours afterwards, just as the regiment marched. The hospital men had no time to stretch him, and he was laid in the earth in the same posture in which he died, with his arms stuck a kimbo, pressing upon his stomach, which shews that he must have suffered intense agony. Poor fellow! they had not time to dig his grave very deep, and I am afraid the jackals will be the only benefiters by his death. We left this place the next morning, the 30th, and arrived here

(Tatta) about eleven o'clock, a twelve-mile march. A great number of the 2nd brigade rode out to meet us, and the 4th Light Dragoons very kindly asked us to breakfast immediately on our arrival. You may be sure they had not to ask us twice!

Tatta is a very ancient town, said to have been built by either Alexander, on his march down the Indus, or by one of his generals; the ancient name was Patala. At that time the country was in possession of Hindoos, or, at least, of the followers of Brahma, who were most probably the original possessors of the greater portion of the east. Afterwards, on the rise of Mahomet, it was soon in possession of his followers, who seem to have held it for a long period, as they have left magnificent proofs of their grandeur, both in the city and all round the neighbourhood, which is studded with splendid cupolas, domes, temples, and tombs; there is one in particular in the town itself, an old tomb, now used as a caravanserai, which is excessively handsome. When I talk of a tomb being turned into a caravanserai, you will of course understand that a tomb in this part of the world is very different from one in the western part of the globe. This tomb itself would cover as much ground as Exeter Cathedral. The inside of the domes are very beautifully enamelled in the chastest colours, and with most excellent taste, and would put to shame the most handsome drawing-room in London, I should think. I have never repented not being able to draw so much as I have since I have been in the East, but particularly since I have been at this place, where there is so much that would look well in a sketch; but I would not give twopence to be able to draw and not draw well, particularly when I see the daubs that some men, who fancy they are hands at it, produce, after fagging at the simplest thing possible, and I believe that if nature does not give you a turn for it, all the trying possible would never make a painter, and that what the old Roman proverb said of the poet, "Non fit sed nascitur poeta," is equally applicable to the painter. I tried it for a short time, at Hanover, but my master told me I was the most awkward and stupid pupil he ever had, and advised me to cut the concern, and I followed his advice; nor am I sorry that I did so, as I should never have been able to draw well, and should have only been discontented, and given it up in disgust. We have, however, two officers in our regiment who both draw and sketch exceedingly well; and I will try to get duplicates from them if possible, so that, if God spares my life, and I ever return home, I shall be able to shew you some specimens of the country we have passed through.

Jan. 2nd.—Well, we are to have no fighting, at least at present, it appears. This will be cheering news for Kitty, I expect. We were most egregiously disappointed in the town or city of Tatta itself. We saw it at a great distance on our march, and on arriving on our encamping ground, it looked excessively well, and gave us the idea of a very handsome place. We saw what we imagined to be high houses, built of stone, towers and pillars; but lo! when we rode in to examine it, these splendid buildings turned out to be a most miserable collection of white mud houses, which had the appearance of stone at a distance. Some of them were tolerably high, certainly; but the most wretched-looking things possible. This is the case with most towns in the east. Like Dartmouth, they all look best à la distance.

I am sorry to say that we have a great many men in the hospital now, and four officers on the sick list; two of them very unwell. All the cases are bowel complaints, and most of them dysentery. This is the case generally. While on the march, soldiers seldom feel it; but when the halt afterwards comes, then they get touched up awfully. However, it is not to be wondered at, when one considers the quantity of duty which they have to perform at present. Out-lying and in-lying pickets, and guards, &c.; add to which, the being suddenly transported from the climate of India, to which most of them have become inured by a residence, on the average, of twelve years, to this comparatively cold and changeful climate, is enough of itself to shake them a little. They have also done what no Indian troops have done before: in marching in India, almost everything is carried for the soldier; he merely carries what he does on parade—viz., his firelock and accoutrements. Our regiment though, by-the-bye, has always carried a blanket, with a clean shirt and stockings and flannel waistcoat wrapped up in it, that they may be enabled to change as soon as they have marched in. On this march, each man has carried his knapsack, with his kit in it, twenty rounds of ammunition, a havresack with his day's rations, and a small round keg containing water, the weight of all which is no joke. While at Bominacote, we fully expected to have a little fighting after passing Tatta, and on our arrival here we heard a report which induced us to believe that we should have a brush with the Ameers very shortly; but it appears now that the Ameers have seen the folly of such proceedings, and have determined to receive us amicably, and to assist our passage through their country, and that it was only one of the Ameers that was inclined to be restive. He endeavoured to stop our camels, &c., and managed to do so for some time, and collected as much of what they call an army as he could—about 5000 of these Beloochees, but with no guns, or anything of that sort. However, on collecting them, they represented to him that the British troops were behaving so well, and the inhabitants of the country were getting so much more money for their articles of sale than they ever got before, that they considered it was more for their profit and advantage that the English should march through their country than that they should oppose them, and get licked into the bargain, as they were sure they would be. All eastern nations have an awful dread of European artillery. It also happened that the poor Ameer had unfortunately not the wherewithal to carry on the war, and his army made excessively high demands on him, you may be sure. The consequence of all which was, that the army dissolved itself as quietly as possible, and the poor Ameer found himself solus. The result is, that a deputation is now here, with a small force from the head Ameer, at Hydrabad, under the command of Nûr Mahomed, another Ameer, and that he has made most ample apologies for the conduct of his brother Ameer, and offered not only to let us pass through his country, but to assist us in so doing to the utmost of his power. It was indeed well for the Ameers that they came to this decision, as had they acted contrary we should have taken possession of their country to a moral certainty. Now they have a chance of keeping half the loaf.

We have here certainly the flower of the Bombay army, and a very respectable force in every respect: two of the best European regiments, four of the best native, the 4th dragoons, two regiments of light cavalry, two troops of horse artillery in prime order, and a battalion of foot artillery, together with a splendid band of auxiliary horse from Cutch, the finest looking fellows I ever saw: they arrived here on the same day as ourselves. I was standing on one of the hills as they wound their way round it; I was never struck with anything so much, nor have I ever seen anything so orientally military before. They are dressed in green garments, edged with gold, and red turbans, tied under the chin, like the old Mahratta soldiers; their arms are match-lock, lance, scimitar, and pistols, and they appear to be excellent and practical riders. They are quite an independent corps, each man finding his own horse, arms, accoutrements, &c., and they take good care to be excellently mounted. They have a few European officers attached to them from the Bombay establishment. Their dress is also uncommonly handsome; a green hussar dress, with gold braiding. In addition to all this force, we have a subsidiary one nearly as large, coming on directly to follow our steps, and occupy Sinde, while we march on with the Bengalees for Cabool. This force, they say, is to consist of H. M. 40th regiment from Deesa, the 10th, 16th, 22nd, and 24th regiments, 23rd N. I., together with H. M. 90th and 61st regiments, and Ceylon Rifle Corps (Malays) from Ceylon, so that I expect the government at home will have to send more regiments to India as quickly as possible. Sir J. Keane is very likely to have the command of the whole force, both Bombay and Bengal, as they say Sir H. Fane is gone back to Bengal with half the Bengal force, in consequence of the Burmese declaring war; which, as might have been expected, they did directly when so many regiments were marched from their neighbourhood. This report is, however, contradicted, and they say now that Sir H. Fane is going home, and will meet us at Shikarpoor or Hydrabad, give up the command to Sir J. Keane, and go down the Indus, and thence to England overland. Which is the true version I know not; but I am afraid that I have little chance of meeting Colonel Fane, and giving him Arthur's letter, which I expected to do when I wrote last. I am delighted at the prospect of our going to Cabool: there we may have some fighting, and have a chance of being permanently quartered till we return to Europe, whenever that may be.

What the original cause of all this was, as I told you before, I hardly know; and you are more likely to get at the true version from some of the Indian newspapers, or from any friends you may have connected with this part of the world, than from me. But, as far as I can learn, this appears to be it: Shah Shooja is the rightful heir to the throne of Cabool, and Dost Mahomed is what Mr. C. Dickens calls the "wrongful one," alias the usurper. Dost Mahomed had possession of the country, and the Indian government, from what motives I know not, determined to unseat him and replace Shah Shooja. In this matter they are assisted by old Runjet Sing, King of Lahore, or, as his oriental title goes, "the blind lion of the Punjab." The Persians, on the contrary, took part with Dost Mahomed, insulted our resident at their court, and besieged Shah Shooja's party in Herat; from which, however, after a siege of long duration, they were finally obliged to retire. There was a report at first that Russia was concerned in this affair, and that Russian troops were present with the Persians at the siege; but these turned out to be a regiment or two of Russian renegadoes whom the King of Persia has in his pay. There was another report of a letter having been discovered from the government of Russia to the King of Persia, which induced the belief that the Emperor of Russia was playing a deep game, the object of which was to lessen our influence in the East; and many people, I believe, are very much of this opinion. How far all this may be true I know not; but I have been told by old Indians that for a long time the Indian government have been anxious to have a strong footing in Sinde, and to command the navigation of the Indus; and that now they have the opportunity they are not likely to let it slip. The Afghans are a very hardy race of men, and we may have some sharp work with them; but I think a gun or two of our horse artillery would have sent the Beloochees scampering. They are miserably equipped; but being nearly all robbers, they might have annoyed us by a night attack, which would have been anything but pleasant, particularly for the poor sub. on out-lying picket. Some Bombay native merchants are at present at Tatta; they have been here for ten years, and have been afraid to stir for fear of being robbed. I have no doubt but that the inhabitants of the country would prefer our government considerably to that of the Ameers, as they are exceedingly tyrannical, and grind their subjects to the last degree, demanding half of everything that is offered for sale. When Burnes travelled first in this country, some few years ago, and was received by the Ameer in divan, at Hydrabad, an old priest who was present is said to have reproved the Ameer for receiving Burnes so civilly, and to have told him "that since one Englishman had seen the Indus, it would not be long before they would be in possession of it;" and so it seems likely to turn out.

Well; as long as I keep my health I care little where we go or what we do; but marching in ill health is a great damper to the spirits. The stay-at-home soldiers in England little know what service in this climate really is. I should like to see ******** of the ***** on out-lying picket here; he would not find it quite so pleasant as Almack's. I have very little time to add more, as the post goes to Bombay to-day, but to wish you all at home a very happy new year, and love to all relations and friends, as you may not hear from me again for some time. I will endeavour to pick up as many curiosities and things of that description as possible for you, if I do not get knocked on the head. I keep a journal, and will write by every opportunity. Your next letter to me may find me in Cabool. Once more, good bye.

Ever your affectionate son,

T. W. E. Holdsworth.

LETTER IV.

Camp, near Jarruk, on the banks of the Indus,
Twenty miles from Hydrabad,
January, 31st, 1839.

My dear Father,—I had fully intended this letter for Kitty, but such a dreadful event happened in our regiment yesterday, that I was afraid, if she was at all unwell when she received the letter, connecting it, as she would, with me, it might throw her into some dreadful fever, or something of that sort. I have very little time to write, as the post leaves this, by steamer, at three o'clock to-day; and I have a great deal to do during the day. I think it my duty, however, to write, as the report of the circumstance might get into the papers without mentioning names, or giving wrong ones, and you might be needlessly alarmed.

To strike at once *in medias res*, this event is no less than the horrible death of three of our officers in a burning shikargur, or large thicket, enclosed by the Ameers for the preservation of game. The names of the poor, unfortunate fellows are Sparke, (whom, by-the-bye, you might have seen at Chatham,) Nixon, and Hibbert. The two first, Lieut. Sparke, in the Grenadiers, and Nixon, in the Light Company. Hibbert was assistant-surgeon. They were three of the finest hearted fellows: Nixon, a long time one of my fellow subs in the Light Company. (I can hardly write, my hand shakes so.) Poor Hibbert was an exceedingly clever fellow, and a great traveller, and one of the most beautiful draughtsmen you could meet with any where. They are all three a terrible loss to our corps. I will tell you the mournful tale as it happened. We arrived here on the 25th. I breakfasted on Tuesday with them at mess, which was the last time I ever saw them alive: they were in exceedingly high spirits. The success of an enterprise the day before appears to have determined them to go upon another expedition on this day, which at first sight did not appear half so hazardous as it unfortunately proved to be; this was no less than going into a shikargur (of which I have explained the meaning above) about four or five miles in the rear of our camp, and which was supposed to be well stocked with game. It happened that this jungle had been set on fire about two days previously, most likely by some of our camel drivers, or other native followers: some said it was done by the Beloochees; but this I think very unlikely, as it is dead to leeward of our camp. Well, they did not appear in the evening, and we began to be rather alarmed on their account: however, we thought they would turn up by some chance or other. Next morning (yesterday), when the regiment fell in, an hour before daylight, which the whole camp does here every morning, as we are supposed to have a hostile force not very far from us, they were reported absent. Breakfast came; no tidings of them: ten; eleven o'clock; and they began to be the talk of the whole camp. However, we speculated that the worst that could have happened to them was being taken prisoners by a party of Beloochees, and kept as hostages, or something of that sort. At twelve, General Willshire became so alarmed and anxious about them that he sent out a troop of the 1st Light Cavalry to scour the jungles, and discover what they could of them; another officer sent out a party of six natives, with the promise of a reward of two hundred rupees if they could find any tidings of them. Well; the day went on; and at mess, at six o'clock, nothing had been heard relative to their fate, except that a little dog belonging to poor Nixon returned to camp about four o'clock. About eight o'clock I was in Dickinson's tent, smoking a cheroot, &c., previous to turning in, when one of our servants rushed in with the dreadful intelligence that the bodies had been found in the jungle by the Light Cavalry. It struck us at first so unexpectedly, and as being a thing so dreadful, that we would hardly believe it; however, all doubt was soon changed into horrible reality by the arrival of the bodies within our lines. I was determined not to see them; but there was a horrible fascination which drew one along with the rest to the hospital tent, where they were lying. * * * * * Twelve o'clock.—Well; I am just returned from seeing the last honours paid to their remains; it is a melancholy business a military funeral; every officer in camp attended; and, after all, they have had the satisfaction of a Christian burial, which may not be our luck in a short time. I do not know why, but this sad event has made me an old woman almost! They lie side by side on a hill just in the rear of our camp; "no useless coffin enclosed their corse;" but there they lie together, wrapped in their cloaks. Peace to their manes! We intend erecting a monument to them, if possible. I learned that some of the staff had been to the jungle to investigate it thoroughly to-day, and from various circumstances, have come to the conclusion that they had climbed up some high trees, which surrounded the place where they fell, in order to shoot the game as they came out, and that before they had time to make their escape, a breeze came, which brought the smoke, and which most likely stifled, or at least rendered them senseless. Let us hope that this was the case, as I should think that so their death would not have been very painful: the position in which their bodies were lying when found seems to warrant this supposition. A porcupine was found close to their trees, burnt to a cinder. It blew very hard last night, and I passed an almost sleepless night in thinking of these poor fellows. It gives a man an awful shake in going through life, seeing the very fellows you have lived with for the last two years, in whose proceedings you have borne a part, brought suddenly before you in such a state: a man in these situations thinks more in two hours than he does in the whole course of his natural life under ordinary circumstances. It proves what helpless beings we are; how little we can control our own actions: truly, "in the midst of life we are in death."

I wrote to you on the new year's day everything that had happened up to that time; the letter was to have gone by the overland mail of the 19th. I hope you will receive it safe, as I should be sorry you should lose anything from me now, as it may be the last you may ever have, so precarious are the chances of a soldier's life on actual service. Shortly after writing to you, I got ill again, and it ended in a slight fever, which cleared me out altogether, since which I have been in perfectly good health, thank God. I came off the sick list on the 22nd January, the day before we marched from Tatta. I will give you my journal from that time to the sad event which has just happened.

Wednesday, Jan. 23, 1839.—On this day, at 6 A.M., the corps d'armé of Sinde marched out of the encampment near Tatta *en route* for Hydrabad, the Cutch Auxiliary Horse in advance, detaching flankers,

&c., then the main body in the following order:— The 4th Light Dragoons in front; next, one squadron of horse artillery, followed by two squadrons of the 1st regiment of Bombay Light Cavalry, one company of foot artillery, then the first brigade of infantry, under General Willshire, consisting of the Queen's Royals, 5th and 1st, or Grenadier regiment, Native Infantry, a second squadron of horse artillery, a second company of foot artillery; the 2nd infantry brigade, consisting of H. M. 17th regiment, the 19th and 23rd regiments Native Infantry; the whole closed by two other squadrons of 1st Light Cavalry. We (i. e., the 1st brigade) left our ground a quarter before six, and halted on a rising ground close to the walls of Tatta, whence we had a very fair view of the cavalry, artillery, &c., that were in the advance of us, winding their way through a pretty avenue of trees: the whole presented a very animated and martial appearance, the different corps marching off with colours uncased, band playing, &c. Cunningham's, or the Poonah Auxiliary Horse, having only arrived the night before, did not join the main body, but came up somewhat later in the day, I believe. The march of the main body this day was not more than ten miles; but our brigade was posted two miles in advance of the rest of the force, and the Queen's were nearly a mile in advance of the other two regiments of the brigade; so that we marched about thirteen miles. We encamped in a rather pretty valley surrounded by barren rocks, with our right resting on a shikargur (or hunting thicket); we had a fine pebbly bottom, which was a great relief to our feet after the hot dust of Tatta. My baggage did not make its appearance till about five o'clock, my unfortunate young camel having proved restive, and flung its load two or three times, thereby considerably damaging my cot and table: mess at six, —nothing particular.

Thursday, Jan. 24.—In consequence of our being so much in advance, our "rouse" did not sound till six o'clock this morning, and we did not march off our ground till seven. After we had marched about two miles, we halted and piled arms, to enable the cavalry, &c., in our rear to pass on, and thus we had a very good review of them: they marched in the same order as yesterday, except that in addition, and near to the light cavalry, came Cunningham's horse from Poonah: this was the first time we had seen them; they made a very splendid appearance, about 600 strong, and well equipped in every respect; their dress and accoutrements the same as the Cutch Horse, (of which I gave you a description in my last,) with the difference of wearing yellow and red instead of green and red. We had a very pleasant march this day, except the latter part, which was exceedingly dusty; some very pretty and romantic scenery, consisting of ruined forts, abrupt hills, large rocks, interspersed with some beautiful lakes here and there. We reached our encamping ground rather late—half-past eleven o'clock—

lost my breakfast, owing to my native groom, who carried some stock for me, and to whom I had given directions to wait by the regiment till they had piled arms and were dismissed, having disobeyed my orders, and cut off with my tatter to the river, about three miles off: gave chase directly the parade was dismissed, and walked through a shikargur to the river, but could not find the rascal. I had, however, a good view of the Indus, which does not here appear to be very broad: a cruel hot day; and, in addition to my other misfortunes, was nearly stifled by the clouds of dust raised by cavalry of every description leading their horses to water. On my return to camp I luckily found my baggage arrived, and had a good snoose till six o'clock, mess time; heard at mess that the Ameers had agreed to all our terms, and would do everything to assist our passage through their country; that we were to march straight to Shikarpoor, without halting at Hydrabad; after remaining at which place for some time, we should advance upon Candahar,—all fudge. Our position this halt was about the centre of the army,—bad encamping ground,—very dusty.

Friday, 25th.—Left our encampment at six, in the same order as before; our out-lying picket, under Stisted, joined us near our first halt, about three miles. Warlike news,—the Ameers had rejected our treaty, and that a force of 10,000 Beloochees had crossed the river, and would probably give us some trouble. Stisted had received orders to keep a very sharp lookout with his picket, as there was a chance of its being attacked: Jephson joined, with news from Sir J. Keane, that there was every chance of our being attacked on the line of march; however, we were not, although we passed over some very pretty ground for a battle. Marched into our encamping ground about half-past ten, near a half-ruined village called Jarruk, on the banks of the river; the army here took up a rather strong position, on a chain of heights; our brigade being, however, pushed on again in advance, on some low and jungly ground near the river; the Queen's again on the extreme front. News still warlike; the Beloochees, under Meer Mahomet, one of the Ameers, and the most restive of them, being supposed to be near us in great force, though nobody seemed to know where. All the oot-wallas, or camel-drivers, put under charge of sentries, as there was reason to suspect they meditated deserting in the night with our camels. Bad encamping ground again,—a dusty, half-cultivated field.

Saturday, 26th.—Turned out of bed between two and three, A. M., with orders to fall in, at a moment's notice, in "light marching order," as an attack was strongly expected. Spies had reported that 10,000 Beloochees were in a shikargur not seven miles from us, and that they intended a night attack; everybody in the highest state of excitement, pistols loading, &c. Fell in an hour before daylight; cavalry sent out in all directions; staff and field-officers galloping about like mad fellows; remained under arms till day had fully broke, when we were dismissed, but commanded not to stray far from camp: great excitement all day; Cunningham's horse sent out to reconnoitre; returned late at night, reporting that they had patrolled sixteen miles in advance, had closely examined the shikargur in question, and could find no traces of the Beloochees, —a strong suspicion, however, remained that there were Beloochees in our neighbourhood.

Sunday, 27th.—Under arms an hour before daylight; no further news; camp quiet. As I was to be on out-lying picket this evening, rode out after breakfast to look at my ground, which appeared rather strong, intersected with ravines, brushwood, &c., and a good place to hold against cavalry. Mounted picket at five o'clock, P. M., fifty-seven rank and file, two serjeants, four corporals, and one bugler, a chain of nine double sentries, the right resting on the river and the Hydrabad road, and the chain running along a dry nullah, till it communicated with the sentries of the 5th regiment's picket; a corporal's party of three men detached in advance to an old ruin on the left front; a picket of cavalry about two miles in advance, with videttes on some high ground. A beautiful moonlight night, and not very cold till about one o'clock in the morning; lay on the ground and thought of what was going on at Brookhill and fancy ball at Torquay; visited my sentries continually; the men in high spirits, and very much on the alert; nothing extraordinary occurred.

Here I have brought my journal down to the sad event which has filled the former part of my letter. With regard to our future operations, reports seem to be so very various that one hardly knows what to think; but the general opinion seems to be, that, as the Ameers still continue restive, Hydrabad will be invested, and, consequently, laid siege to in due form in a few days. We intend, I believe, to cross the river here, and not further up, where we should be exposed to the fire of the Beloochees, who muster pretty strong there. We are only waiting for our gun-boats, they say, which take a long time to come up, and move about the rate of two miles a day, owing to the strong current. The report to-day is, that a force is to be detached to this place from the Bengal army at Shikarpoor, as we are not strong enough to invest Hydrabad by ourselves, and we must not give the enemy the slightest chance of success, as the influence our arms have must be supported, otherwise we may be deserted by our native army. I wish something had been definitely settled by this time; but I must not lose this steamer, otherwise I might not have a chance of writing again. The overland sails on the 21st proximo: I hope this will reach you safe. Tell Kitty I received her letter, dated October 1st, while at Tatta, and cannot tell how it was that she did not receive any from me for five months, as I wrote in June; but several officers have heard from their friends that their letters have been missing about that time, and I am afraid that a mail has been lost. I do not think that the Ameers would oppose us of themselves, but they cannot control their army, these robber Beloochees, who do pretty much what they like, and have it their own way everywhere; if defeated, they can easily retreat to their mountain hold, the Lukke mountains, separating Beloochistan from Sinde. With best love to all at home, and with every hope that they may escape the chances and perils to which we poor soldiers are exposed,

Believe me, ever your most affectionate son,

T. W. E. Holdsworth.

LETTER V.

Camp Kotree, four miles from Hydrabad,
February 6th, 1839.

MY DEAR FATHER,—I wrote to you a few days ago from Jarruk, informing you of the melancholy fate of three of my brother officers; but having received your letter since, dated Nov. 20th, containing the bill for 670 rupees (or 70*l.*), and informing me of the news of Kate's intended marriage, I could not let slip an opportunity which has just occurred, by our having got possession of Curachee, of writing to Kitty, and also, at the same time, of informing you of what has occurred since. You will receive this at the same time as you do the other, since it will arrive at Bombay in time to go by the same overland mail.

I wrote to you on the 31st; and on Sunday, the 3rd of February, we marched out of Jarruk for this place; we made a two days' march of it, both very disgusting; horrible, or rather no roads at all; nothing but dust and sand under our feet, which the wind blew into our eyes every minute; add to which, small halts every five minutes, on account of the artillery in our front, who could not get on through the badness of the way: this perpetual halting is the most wearisome thing possible to a soldier when once fairly under weigh. Well; we arrived here on the day before yesday; our front is now completely changed, being towards the river, and not turned from it, or with our right resting on it, as it has been before; our brigade is on the extreme right. Of course, you know that we are on the western bank, and that Hydrabad is on the eastern, and therefore the opposite one. Since we have been here, we have a little relaxed in our discipline, being no longer under arms before daylight; but reports are still very various as to whether we are to have peace or war with the Ameers, and whether we shall eventually have to sack Hydrabad or not. A deputation from thence came over yesterday to Sir J. Keane. It appears that the Ameers will agree to our treaty, but demur about the money which that treaty obliges them to pay. As far as I can learn, though I do not advise you to put much reliance on it, as I may very likely be wrong, this seems to be the case. It appears that the Ameers have long owed our ally, whom we are going to place on the throne of Cabool, Shah Shooja, twenty lacs of rupees; that on our declaring war they agreed to pay this sum, with Shah Shooja's consent, to our government to meet the expenses of the war, and to give us a passage through their country to Shikarpoor. However, from our first landing in their country they have played a most underhand game, and endeavoured to throw every indirect obstacle in our way, behaving friendly to our faces, but behind our backs giving very different directions to their satellites: this was found out by means of intercepted letters, particularly at our last halt at Jarruk. The conduct of our party may not be considered of quite the fairest nature, as we are establishing posts in their country by way of communication, and reserves at three or four different places. This was, no doubt, part of the original plan that sent us here, as these posts are to be strongly fortified, consisting, it is supposed, of Shikarpoor, Schwun, Tatta, and Curachee, and are to be the posts of defence on our north-west frontiers against any incursions from our northern neighbours, particularly Russia. The Ameers are particularly indignant at this, as I am told it did not form part of the original treaty, and they see in it, no doubt with justice, a prelude to our final possession of their country. Pottinger, the political agent, had collected, before he left Hydrabad, grain for the army to the value of three lacs of rupees; this, it is now found out, has either been taken away or destroyed, and Sir J. Keane immediately added it to the other twenty lacs contained in the treaty. The Ameers say they will pay half the whole sum demanded here, and the remaining half on our arrival at Shikarpoor.

This Sir J. Keane has refused, and told them he will not leave this or Hydrabad till he gets every fraction.

We yesterday received news which must, I should think, have an effect on the Ameers one way or the other. The admiral on this station, Sir F. Maitland, brought up in his 74 (I think the Wellesley) H. M. 40th regiment, from Mandivie, in Cutch, to Curachee, a fort on the westernmost branch of the Indus. On approaching the fort, the Beloochees who garrisoned it, taking it for a common free-trader, had the foolish presumption to fire into her; the admiral wore his vessel round, just gave one broadside, down came their fort in one second about their ears,—you may guess how it astonished them: they sent word to say that the English fire a lac of shot in one second. They say the Ameers were one year in taking this place, which cost the English one second. I think myself that we shall not have any fighting here, and that Hydrabad will still remain in the hands of the Ameers.

The report to-day is, that we cross the river to-morrow; if so, I suppose with hostile intentions, or at least for intimidation; but this I hardly believe. Sir J. Keane, they say, refused to receive the deputation from the Ameers yesterday. Should the thing be settled peaceably, we shall immediately march for Shikarpoor, and thence most likely on Candahar, a new climate. It has been getting gradually hotter here; and in the hot season Sinde is dreadful.

At Shikarpoor we meet a part, if not the whole, of the Bengal force, and Shah Shooja, with his and Runjet Sing's contingent, is also there. Runjet himself is very ill: part of the agreement between him and us was, that we should preserve the throne to his son on his demise. He was excessively civil to Lord Auckland, and all the English who have been at Lahore. Sir H. Fane, they say, still proceeds with the Bengal army. The drummer is here waiting for my letter, as it is very late for the post, so, in haste, good bye. Love, &c., and believe me ever,

Your most affectionate son,

T. W. E. Holdsworth.

P.S. Jephson is post-master to the force.

LETTER VI.

Camp, near Larkhanu,
Wednesday, 6th March, 1839.

My dear Father,—I last wrote to you from Kotree, opposite Hydrabad. We are now, as you will see by the date, at Larkhanu, a pretty considerable distance from the former place. I see, by my journal, that it was the 6th of February when I last wrote, exactly one month ago. We were then, I believe, rather ignorant of what the Ameers intended; but the fate of Curachee, of which I gave you an account, brought them to their senses, and the day after I wrote things were settled, and officers had permission to visit Hydrabad, merely reporting their names to their respective majors of brigade before they did so. In consequence of which I went over to that place on the 9th, with Dickenson and Piercy; but there was not much to repay us for our ride, under a cruelly hot sun, as the fort, the only place worth seeing, was shut up, and no one could get a view of the inside except a few of the staff. It did not appear to be very strong, although it had a pretty appearance. I think the Ameers acted very wisely, as it could easily be taken by escalade. The rest of the town consisted of a great straggling bazaar, just the same as is to be seen everywhere in India; and it did not appear a bit better than that at Belgaum. There were some fine elephants belonging to the Ameers, and some pretty ruins on the outskirts of the town. The Beloochees had all left, and were nowhere to be seen.

Sunday, the 10th, we marched off our ground at Kotree, and reached Lukkee on Saturday, the 16th, after a six days' march, most of them fifteen miles. Here we halted four days to allow the pioneers, &c., to make a road over the Lukkee Pass for the artillery. We found here some excellent sulphur springs and baths, about a mile from our encampment, among the Lukkee hills, which, if they could be transported to Dartmouth, would make a second Bath of it. The whole of our force were bidetizing here all day long. Being so directly under the hills, we found it rather warmer than we liked. There were some large lakes here, full of wild duck, and capital partridge-shooting, and we were cracking away all the time. On the march to this place I had the misfortune to lose a very nice little bull-terrier bitch, about a year old, which I had from a pup, at Belgaum, and which had followed my fortunes so far. It was all her own fault, as she broke from my tent one night, and though I used every endeavour I could hear nothing more of her.

The 21st we marched over the Pass to Schwun, the largest place in Sinde next to Tatta. The Pass was not half so bad as we expected, so we filed over it very easily. On our arrival at Schwun we heard that Sir H. Fane had just passed down the river, with his staff, *en route* for Bombay, and was laying at anchor about five miles down the river, where Sir J. Keane went to meet him; so that here ended my last chance of meeting Col. Fane, and giving him Arthur's letter. Sir H. Fane will remain at Bombay, which is to be the head quarters of the Indian army while this business lasts. We only halted one day at Schwun; I rode in to look at the town, which was nearly desolate, as the inhabitants of every place invariably remove with their families on our arrival. There was, however, a fine old castle in ruins, which was well worth seeing, and must have been a place of some importance in former days; and a very superb mosque in the centre of the town, in which was a tame tiger. We left Schwun on Saturday, the 23rd, crossing the Arrul river, which flows round the town into the Indus, on pontoons, and commenced our first march in Upper Sinde. This day's march was delightful, and the only tolerable one we have had, all the rest being through a dismal, dusty desert, with sometimes no path at all, and the dust generally so thick in marching that you cannot see an inch before you. This was, however, a grand exception. We marched by the side of a magnificent lake, full of wild fowl, the banks of which were carpeted with rich wild clover, and over-shadowed with fine trees, the only ones of any size that we have yet seen in Sinde; so that you might almost fancy you were going through a nobleman's park in England (Kitly, par example.) In fact, this place put me more in mind of Old England than any I have seen in the East. From Schwun we marched direct to this place, which we reached on the 4th, the day before yesterday, without halting once: most of the marches fifteen miles, and all terrible teasers, on account of the badness of the roads, and the stupidity or wilful ignorance of our guides. One of our marches was to have been a short one of ten miles; but for some unaccountable reasons our route and encamping ground were changed three times. We lost our way in the jungle, and marched fifteen, instead of ten, miles before we found ourselves in our proper places; on arrival at which we found that half the officers' and men's baggage was gone on to our next encamping ground, fifteen miles further, which, owing to the variety of places named in orders, our servants supposed to be the right one. My baggage was one of the unlucky; but my servant came back with my things about five o'clock in the evening; so that my poor camels must have gone nearly forty miles that day, with a prospect of another fifteen the next morning at five. General Willshire, and, I hear,

Sir J. Keane also, were among the sufferers. Our poor sick were all lost in the jungles for this day, and we saw nothing of half of them till we arrived on our next encamping ground. Some of them were upwards of twenty-four hours without getting anything to eat, or attendance of any sort. Well, we marched to this place on the day before yesterday, after ten days' regular hard work. A great number in hospital; though they are coming out again now pretty fast.

It is believed we shall halt here about a week; but what we shall do then nobody seems to know. The greater part of the force will, it is believed, follow the Bengalees to Candahar, who marched from Shikarpoor for that purpose, under Sir Willoughby Cotton, on the 22nd, but have since been detained, owing to the impracticability of the country. One regiment of our brigade (the Grenadier regiment, Native Infantry) is under orders for Bukkur, an island fort on the Indus, about twenty-five miles from Shikarpoor, which (i. e., Bukkur) is to be our depôt for stores, &c., and where all the present unfits, in the shape of sick men, are to be sent. No doubt some other troops will be left in Upper Sinde, at different places, and I have some fears that the "Queen's" may be among the number. Heaven defend us from being quartered in any part of this wretched country, particularly from Shikarpoor, which is said to be one of the hottest places in existence. In fact, the Persians say,

"While there is a Shikarpoor, there ought to be no Johannum," or hell. What a pity it would be to lose such a capital chance of seeing Candahar, and perhaps Cabool, which is said to be a splendid place and a delightful climate. The Bolan Pass, a most magnificent and difficult one, the key to Afghanistan from Sinde, is said to be now totally impassable, from the number of dead cattle, horses, and camels, which Shah Shooja's force lost there. This I believe, however, to be mere report. We heard, the other day, that Dost Mahomed had occupied it, and that we should have to take it at the point of the bayonet. So much do reports vary, one knows not what to believe. This pass, said to be thirty miles long, and at some places almost impassable, runs through and over the large chain of mountains that separates the mountainous country of Candahar and Cabool, or, as it is generally called, Afghanistan, from the lowland of Sinde; it is not easy to cross it, at least before April, as till then the snows are not melted.

I hope and trust my next letter will be dated from Candahar, which is, however, a good six weeks' march from this place. We have found the weather dreadfully hot for the last few days, averaging generally 106 in our tents in the day time, though the nights are cool, and the mornings generally very cold. I have not yet been in Larkhanu, though we marched through a part of it on our arrival. Our men have been now for three days without any dram at all, and their rations are getting worse and worse every day; in fact, things are so bad that they have been obliged to send to Shikarpoor for part of what was left there by the Bengal commissariat, which is said to be excellent, and which has fed their army very well, although they have come a much greater distance than we have.

I spoke to our paymaster about my bill, and he has shewn it to the paymaster-general, who says he will cash it whenever I like, but that I must take it in a lump; he will not give it me by instalments. This is a great nuisance, as it is very hazardous taking so much money about with one; the money, too, takes up a great deal of room and is very heavy; it was, however, quite a god-send, as I had no idea how very expensive this march would turn out; grain for cattle being exceedingly dear, the natives raising the price to about 500 per cent. everywhere, thanks to bad management somewhere. At Tatta each officer received a month's pay in advance, that he might purchase cattle for his baggage. This is to be deducted by three instalments, one from each of the next three issues of pay. An ensign's pay for one month will hardly purchase sufficient conveyances. The only mode in this country is by camels, and a camel is of all animals the most treacherous, or rather precarious lived; they get ill suddenly and go off in three hours: a great number have died with us. Now an officer losing his camels loses one month's pay, and must leave his kit on the ground, as he has nothing wherewith to replace his loss. You can, therefore, imagine what a great relief your bill proved to me, as I shall always have it to fall back upon. I bought a very nice little Cabool horse at Kotree, from one of the Ameers' disbanded Beloochees. He is very hardy, and accustomed to this country, and not particular as to his food, which is a capital thing, as most of the Arab horses that have been brought from India have fallen off terribly. He is a very pretty figure, goes well, and leaps capitally, which few of the Arabs can. I gave 170 rupees for him, or 17*l.* In India, I am confident he would fetch 500 or 600 rupees (50*l.* or 60*l.*)

I am very doubtful as to the time when this letter may reach you; I hope it may catch the overland mail on the 25th; but Jephson says it is very doubtful, and will depend entirely on the chance of there being a ship at Curachee, or off the Hujamree. The heat now, while I am writing, is dreadful, and there is a beastly hot wind blowing which I never felt before. Heaven send us soon out of Sinde! We are expecting the overland mail from England every day; it generally manages to come two days after I write home. You will by this time have received the letter I wrote from the Syden, and the one

I wrote to Kate about the 13th of December from Bominacote. Reports vary much as to whether we shall have any fighting if we advance into Candahar. I should think Dost Mahomed would like to try a brush with us, at least with Shah Shooja.

With love to all at home,

Believe me your affectionate son,

T. W. E. Holdsworth.

LETTER VII.

Camp, Candahar, June 8th, 1839.

My dear Father,—I begin this letter to you on the 8th of June, 1839, though when it will reach you, or whether it ever will, is very doubtful. I have not written, I see, since the beginning of March, from Larkhanu; there was, however, very little use in so doing, as there was very little chance of your ever getting it, our friends the Beloochees, Kaukers, &c., having made free with nearly every mail, and destroyed them. I am very much afraid that I also have been a sufferer by them, and that you must have written to me long ere this, but that our friends of the Bolan Pass have made use of the letter to wrap their cabobs in. I have not heard from you or from home at all since the 2nd of February, when I got your letter, dated November 20th, enclosing the bill on government, and informing me of Kate's intended marriage. I have, however, long since this heard of my lieutenancy, and seen my name in the "Gazette," but have not yet received the confirmation of it from Sir H. Fane in this country, so that I have been fighting my way, and am likely to continue so, on the rank and pay of a full ensign; however, there will be so much the more back pay to receive when it does come; it is a great nuisance, however, not having it, as I require it so much in this country. You can form no conception of the hopeless expense which we have inevitably been obliged to incur. We have had a tolerable share of hardships, &c., and the poor marching soldiers have suffered terribly. What do you think of our having made a forced march of thirty to forty miles, for six hours of it under the hottest sun I can recollect, and I have felt a few of them in India? Since we left Larkhanu we have met with little but a series of robberies, murders, alarms, and skirmishes; in short, everything but an actual stand-up fight, which we were all anxious for, as it would settle matters at once, and free us from the predatory attacks and cold-blooded murders of these barbarous tribes.

To begin from where I left off: we marched from Larkhanu on the 11th March, and reached Dadur, about four miles from the entrance to the Bolan Pass, the nest of the robber hordes of Kaukers, Tuckers, and Beloochees, on the 6th of April, having halted several times at intermediate places, and made some terrible marches, fifteen miles being the average distance. We often lost our way, and marched thereby a great deal further than was necessary, through bad guidance. I must tell you, however, that before leaving Larkhanu, Sir J. Keane assumed the command of the whole army, both Bengal and Bombay, by which General Willshire got command of the Bombay division. The two Bombay brigades were broken up, the Grenadiers and 5th regiment of Native Infantry were sent to garrison Bukkur, a tolerably strong fort on the Indus, and the 23rd Native Infantry was sent to Lukkur, a town on the opposite side. There also the different regiments that were to go on sent their sick, and Bukkur was made a depot for supplies, medical stores, &c. The greater part of the foot and some of the horse artillery were sent there also. Our regiment and the 17th were then made into one brigade, and marched from Larkhanu, as I said before, on the 11th. The cavalry and horse artillery, &c., did not march for two days after, with the Commander-in-chief, who took with him his pet corps, the 19th Native Infantry. They marched by a different route from ourselves on account of the scarcity of supplies in that desert country; we halted for them at Kochee, which place we reached on the 15th about 3 P. M., after the thirty to forty miles' march I before told you of, across the marshy desert which seems to divide Sinde from Cutch Gundava. This march ought only to have been twenty-six miles; but owing to the stupidity of our guide we went a longer and more circuitous route, and also had the pleasure of losing our way during the night; in addition to which, on arriving at the village where it was intended to halt, our staff found out, all of a sudden, that there was not a sufficiency of water for the whole force, in consequence of which we were moved to another village (Kichee) five miles further on.

It was during this march that I first witnessed the effects of extreme thirst on men, however well disciplined. It was, as I have said before, the hottest day I ever felt; not a breath of air, and the sun enough to knock you down. The men were suffering dreadfully, and falling out by sections, when about eleven or twelve o'clock they caught sight of some water carriers with their mussacks full, so that they knew water could not be far off. All discipline was pitched to the devil in an instant, and the men rushed from the ranks for the water more like mad devils than anything else—nothing could stop them; the mounted officers galloped in amongst them, and threatened, but to no purpose; nothing short of cutting them down would have stopped any of them. In the midst of this, General Willshire, at the head of the brigade, hearing a row and looking round, saw the greater part of the 17th (they being in front on this day) scampering across the country like a pack of hounds; not knowing what was the matter, he galloped up to the colonel and demanded an explanation, when, seeing what was the cause, he made the best of it, called a halt, and every one immediately rushed to the wells, the scenes at which were most ridiculous, fighting, pushing, knocking down, &c. I saw one man actually lie down and wallow in a filthy ditch full of every description of dirt imaginable. We halted here about two hours, and then marched to our ground, about six or seven miles further on, the men performing this latter part of the march with great cheerfulness. We halted here two days to rest the men, and were joined by the rest of the Bombay force, with the Commander-in-chief.

We marched again on the 18th, another night march about twenty miles. Here we made another halt for three days, while some of the staff went on to get information of the country a-head, about which they were ignorant. All the villages we had passed through were deserted, and in some places the water was stinking. We looked back upon Sinde as a paradise compared to the country we were now in. All the little grain that was supplied to the bazaars by the commissariat was sold at the most exorbitant price, yet we were obliged to buy it, and as much as we could get of it too, and lucky we thought ourselves to get any of it, even at this rate, at times, in order to feed our horses and camels, which were beginning to knock up terribly. We could not now, as we used to do in Sinde, send the latter into the jungle to feed on the small brushwood, of which they were so fond, except at the risk of being robbed of them, and having the servants who looked after them murdered by the bands of Beloochees who hovered about us in every direction. Still, notwithstanding these annoyances, the humbugging system of conciliation was kept up, and although there was not an inhabitant to be seen, we were robbed to our faces very nearly; yet if a poor sub.'s horse or camel happened to break his ropes and strayed into a field he was immediately pounced upon by a provost-marshal and put into a sort of pound, from which he was not released except on the payment of a certain sum to be given to the owners of the field! Where were they to be found? The loss of camels now was irreparable; even if there were any to be sold, the prices asked were so exorbitant that few of us youngsters, hampered as we were, could afford to purchase; loss of camels produced loss of kit, loss of kit produced loss of health, &c. Yet during the whole of this march we were losing camels through robberies and fatigue, and no measures taken that we ever heard of to put a stop to it. We marched from this place on the 22nd, and came to a halt again at a place called Kotrie, close under the Hala mountains, about five miles from the Gundava Pass. Here we (i. e., our brigade and the 4th Light Dragoons) halted for a week. Sir J. Keane pushed on a-head with two troops of Light Cavalry and the left wing of the 19th Native Infantry, in order to catch up Sir Willoughby Cotton, who was marching in command of the main body of the Bengal division. General Willshire, with the staff, artillery, and cavalry, was at Gundava, about eight miles from us. At this place, Kotrie, which the inhabitants luckily had not deserted, we were better off in point of supplies than we had been since we left Larkhanu, and there was plenty of shooting and fishing; but it was without exception the hottest place I ever was in. Being close under a high range of mountains, we were perfectly screened from any cool breezes that might take it into their heads to blow from that quarter; add to this, the hills themselves, being composed of granite, or some stone of that description, attracted the sun, and reflected the heat back again on us, so that we were attacked from two sides at once. By this time we had no stronger liquor with us than tea, so that we were perfectly eligible to become members of the Tea-total Temperance Society; our supplies in the liquor line, which we had sent on from Hydrabad to Larkhanu by water, not having reached the latter place in time for us to get them. In this respect the men were better off than ourselves, they having their dram or two every day. Here the robbers began to be more bold, and we did not lose sight of them until we reached Candahar. Five mails (one of them an "overland," bringing, perhaps, letters from you or some one at home) out of six were robbed between this and Shikarpoor; and news was received from Sir J. Keane in advance that at the entrance of the Bolan Pass several bodies of sepoys of Shah Shooja's army were lying, there having been a grand skrimmage there between the sepoys and Beloochees, in which the former, being caught napping, were worsted. We stayed at this place, as I said before, a week, and started again on the 31st.

On the morning of the 2nd of April, during a severe march of twenty-two miles, one of our men, a straggler, who had fallen to the rear with dysentery, was murdered by these robbers, and another man of the 17th cruelly wounded, but he has since recovered. They were sitting together by the side of the road, when of a sudden a party of Beloochees rushed out from some low bushes, and, before either had time to rise, fired into them. Adams, of the Queen's, received a ball on the outside of his right thigh, passing down, and coming out at his knee on the other side, and cutting some particular vein or artery, which occasioned his death through loss of blood. The 17th man was hit on the right side, the ball coasting round his body, and coming out at the other side, without touching his tripes or any vital part. Adams had not his firelock with him, but the 17th man had his, but unloaded, and, in his struggles to keep possession of it, received some desperate sabre cuts; but he has since recovered. Of course he was soon overpowered, as Adams could give no assistance. The Beloochees then stripped them of everything, except their shirt and trowsers, and left them to their fate, till another man of the 17th came up, in charge of some of his company's camels, who brought in the news to camp; but the apothecary who went out was too late to save poor Adams. It was gratifying to know that Cunningham, with a party of his horse, having received intelligence that a party of these blackguards were encamped in a jungle, beat through it, and followed their tracks for fourteen miles, when he came upon them, and killed six and took four prisoners; Cunningham having outstripped his party, killed two men himself and took another prisoner. These rascals were brought into camp, and strictly guarded, or I believe they would have been torn to pieces by the European soldiers. One of them was sworn to by the wounded 17th man as being one of the murderers, and we were all in great hopes of seeing the blackguards dancing the tight rope; but, instead of that, they were all brought on (except one, who being badly wounded, died on the road) to Dadur, where they were given up to one of the political diplomatic gentlemen, who, it is said, actually let them go with five rupees to carry them home. Fancy a Beloochee's *home!* This was carrying the conciliation principle far with a vengeance!

We started again at half-past twelve, on the night of the 3rd—another night-march of nineteen miles. Both the nights we were at this place we were alarmed by a supposed attack of Beloochees; but they turned out to be nothing more than a loose horse or two of the dragoons, for which one of their camp-followers suffered, being taken for a Beloochee, while running after one of the horses, and therefore cut down by a dragoon on sentry. The night we left this place was one of the most fearful I ever remember; it had been threatening all the afternoon, and about eight the simoom came on with dreadful violence, blowing for five minutes at a time, at intervals of twenty minutes or so, until we got under weigh, at half-past twelve. The wind, hot and scorching, like a blast from a furnace, rushed over the country with the violence of a hurricane, bringing with it perfect clouds of dust and sand, so that it was totally impossible to face it, except at the risk of being actually blinded or stifled. The baggage was to have gone on before us at nine o'clock, as the moon was expected to be up, but the clouds of dust, &c., completely hid her from us, and she did not shew her nose the whole night. During the blasts it was the most perfect "darkness visible" that you can imagine, and at the intervals when it ceased, the sensation of the atmosphere was more like standing before a hot fire than anything else. I had read of these things before in novels, travels, &c; I now, for the first time, experienced the reality. Add to all these little annoyances, we were every moment expecting a rush of Beloochees; and if they had had the pluck of a hare, they might have considerably crippled our proceedings, by rushing in and ham-stringing our camels. The darkness, the unavoidable confusion, the awkwardness of the camels themselves, all favoured them, and I expected nothing less; if they had been Cossacks instead, they would have played the very devil with us altogether. At length, at half-past eleven, the baggage got off, and now for the first time with a baggage guard, consisting of a troop, or company, from each of the three regiments, together with all the irregular horse we possessed, with strict orders that any Beloochees shewing themselves at all near the baggage were instantly to be cut down or bayoneted. The main body followed in another hour, with a strong rear-guard, to pick up stragglers, &c. These precautions ought to have been taken before, and poor Adams would have been saved. I know very little of this march, as I remember I slept through the whole of it, until morning, on horseback, being terribly fatigued and worn out. The morning was delightfully cool, with a fresh bracing breeze from the north. You may well imagine how we enjoyed it, after the terrible relaxation of the night before. We reached our ground about seven, at a place called Nonsherah. Here we heard some bloody-minded reports of the Beloochees, who had been plundering the artillery and left wing of the 19th, which were here the day before. They seemed, however, to have made a pretty good retaliation, and four Beloochees' heads were stuck upon the walls of the town, in proof of the soldiers' vengeance. In consequence of there being a good baggage-guard, the Beloochees made themselves tolerably scarce during this march, although the ground was very favourable for them. However, they now and then took long shots from the nullahs, &c., that were near the road, but without doing any damage. At last, a soldier, from the baggage-guard company of the 17th, having occasion to fall out, and going into a nullah for his purpose, unexpectedly found himself cheek by jowl with thirty of these rascals. He was knocked down, but bellowing out most lustily, his section came up, and being joined by another section of the Queen's, they shot about six of them dead, and put the rest to flight, having rescued the 17th man. The robbers at this place were *rather* forward, and actually walked off with some camels that were out feeding close to the rear of our encampment, in the middle of the day. They were, however, all recovered very soon by the Irregulars, and those of the robbers who could not manage to escape, managed to get their heads broken by these surwars; and intelligence having been received that a whole gang, with their families, were encamped near us, a party of fourteen, and one jemadar, of the 1st Light Cavalry, were sent out, who coming unexpectedly upon them, the robbers advanced to shew fight, when the jemadar gave the word to fire, and each trooper brought down his bird. The rest immediately took to their heels, and owing to the nature of the ground (it was among the hills) effected their escape. The troopers returned to camp with the swords and shields, &c., of the fallen. From this place we marched again the next morning, and a short and easy march brought us to Dadur.

June 27th.—I have not been able to write much lately, as it was literally too hot to do so. We have had it from 115 to 120 in our tents during the day; for the last week, however, it has been getting cooler, and to-day is pleasant enough. I wished also to keep the letter open as long as I could; but now, since we march on Sunday next, the 30th, I have not much time left, though I have a great deal more to say. I received by the mail the confirmation of my lieutenancy, by Sir H. Fane, from Bombay. An "overland" arrived again here last night, but no letters or anything for me. I see, by the English papers, that there was a report at home that we had lost 3000 men already—the greatest lie possible. If we had lost that, we should have lost more than half the Bombay army. We have not lost more than we generally do in quarters, though the men have been terribly knocked up, and well they may be, with the horrible marches they have made. I was very much amused by the debates in Parliament, with regard to our "military promenade," as some of the papers call it. I wish I could see some of their writers on an outlying picket, with a prospect of a twenty miles' march, I rather think they would not talk so much of "promenading." The Bengal army, with our cavalry, and most of the artillery, marched this morning for Cabool. Shah Shooja goes to-morrow or next day, and we bring up the rear, as I said before, on Sunday. However, we will talk of that anon, or I shall forget where

I left off. On looking back, I find that I have brought the force up as far as Dadur. Well; we halted there till the 12th. The 17th, artillery and Irregular Horse, however, marched before us, on the 9th. While there, the rascally Beloochees and Kaukers kept hovering about us, and walked off with some camels and a horse or two. They generally, however, paid very dearly for them, as the cavalry that were sent after them on these occasions made a terrible example of them.

While here we heard of a shocking murder at Curachee. A Captain Hand, of the 1st Bombay Grenadier Regiment, was taking his morning's ride, when, on turning a corner on the top of a hill, he unexpectedly found himself in the midst of about thirty Beloochees. They talked to him very civilly, and he allowed them to get round his horse, not suspecting anything, when one rascal behind him gave him a terrible wipe on the back of his head with his sword, which knocked him off his horse, and the others rushed in, and cut him to pieces. A Lieut. Clarke, of the same corps, happened to be riding this way, and seeing these Beloochees, asked them if they had seen a Latich pass that way, meaning Hand; to which they replied by a volley from their matchlocks, a ball from one of which struck Clarke on the leg, and he galloped for camp as fast as he could, and fell off his horse exhausted before the quarter-guard of H. M. 40th regiment. A party was immediately sent out, and they found the body of poor Hand horribly mutilated. A good number of these rascals have been since taken, and, I suppose, hanged; unless the conciliation principle lets these rascals off also. They belong to different bands, under different robber-chiefs, among the hills. These robber Khans have strongholds on the almost inaccessible mountains that run up the whole west frontier of Sinde, and divide it from Beloochistan. All merchandize and travellers passing through Sinde to the west of the Indus are obliged to pay a sort of black mail to these Khans to be allowed to pass through; but so bad is their name for treachery, ferocity, &c., that few, if any, of the traders between India and Central Asia go this route. They do not care a farthing for the Ameers, who also secretly connive at their proceedings, in order to draw recruits from them on any emergency.

Well; we got the steam up again on the 12th, and, together with the 4th Light Dragoons, and about sixty Irregulars, started for the celebrated Bolan Pass, with a great quantity of commissariat stores from Bukkur, for the army in advance, under our charge. This celebrated Pass would be the best line of communication between the countries of Central Asia and Sinde; and as far as the Pass is concerned itself, it is quite guiltless of the bad character it holds. It is merely the bed of a winter torrent, and is an easy ascent the whole way through; and during the greater part of the year quite passable for any description of conveyance; but in consequence of the great number of robbers, from all parts of Beloochistan and Sinde, who infest it, no one thinks of travelling this route, unless with a very strong escort. A great number, therefore, of native merchants, &c., took advantage of the opportunities offered by the passage of it by the different divisions of our army. We had with us a native horse-dealer, who had travelled the same way down the year before, with horses for the Bombay market, and, as he considered, with a sufficient escort; but they were suddenly attacked, his brother killed, and he only saved himself by the swiftness of his horse. These robbers are several degrees more savage than even their brother Beloochees in the south of Sinde. There are two clans of them. The Kaukers and Tuckers; of these, the Kaukers are by far the worst. They are represented as being regular barbarians, and are even said to be cannibals, though perhaps that is a little too melodramatic. They possess few fire-arms, but roll down large pieces of rock in the narrow passes, and rush out from the small recesses of the rocks, leading God knows where, which abound in every part. They never spare any one, and cut and hack about the bodies of their victims in the most frightful manner. With all this they are the greatest cowards possible; a few determined men would be a match for the greatest odds; but the very name of Kauker seems to convey terror in it to a traveller. I saw the head of one of these rascals lying about at Dadur, and it was the most frightful face I ever beheld, more like a wild beast's than a human being's. On entering the Pass, which we did as if expecting an enemy, with skirmishers, flanking parties, &c., we were nearly stifled by the horrible smell arising from the number of dead camels which were lying on the ground, in every degree of putrefaction. We soon, however, came to bodies of a different sort; for on the banks of a small rivulet, and in the water, most in the long reeds, some in the middle of the road, were about twenty or thirty dead Sepoys and followers. They were in every kind of shape and contortion that could indicate a violent death. Some were in a tolerable state of preservation, but others, again, had been sadly mauled; tripes torn out by jackals, and one or two were perfect skeletons. We kept on coming also upon an arm or a leg, or an ugly-looking skull; but the most disgusting sight was an arm and leg, protruding out of the centre of the stream, washed to the consistency of a washer-woman's hand after a hard day's washing. If you can fancy all this on a dark, sluggish-looking stream, surrounded by high and barren rocks, you may, perhaps, guess what feelings of disgust it excited in us. However, before reaching Candahar we were pretty well accustomed to these sights, and got rather callous on the subject, as there was a fair sprinkling of them to be met with all the way to that town. Well; we made five marches through this delightful Pass, and debouched on a fine wide plain on the 17th. Not a stick, not a particle of forage, except some high rank grass, was to be got in all this time, and we had been obliged to take on supplies for our camels and horses from Dadur; so there was a new expense, and new carriage to be provided. The robbers did not attempt any attack upon us at all (though, if they had had the slightest pluck, they might have crippled us pretty considerably) except in the last march, but then we fired on them first. My company was on baggage-guard this day, which was sent on in advance of the column; and Halket, seeing some of the rascals on the hills, had a crack at them with his double-barrel, which produced a reply of three shots from them; but a soldier of the company taking a beautiful aim at one of them, at a distance I am afraid to mention, and nearly knocking a fellow's head off, the rest took to their heels, and we saw no more of them. Our Grenadiers, however, who were bringing up the rear, had a slight skrimmage with them, and killed five or six, without any of their shots taking effect, although one man's firelock and another man's belt were cut in half by a bullet. They fired on the column which came on afterwards, and wounded one trooper of the Light Dragoons, and a few native followers, and killed three horses. Most of us lost a deal of kit in this Pass, owing to the camels' feet knocking up, from the sharpness of the stones; and the very moment the column was off the ground the rascals would be down and fighting for what was left behind. I was on rear-guard the second day's march, and the very moment we cleared the ground it was most amusing to see the rascals popping out of the holes in the rocks in every direction.

On the 18th, we reached Siriab, where we halted for one day. This was a rather pretty valley, with some fruit gardens, but the fruit not ripe. Here I was taken unwell, and obliged to go on the sick-list; I had been ailing some time; the doctor, however, put me off the list again on the 24th; but owing to the fatigue &c. I underwent on 25th, in going through the Ghwozhe Pass, I caught a violent fever, and the next day was laid on my beam ends, and did not get round again till the middle of last month. In the Ghwozhe Pass our company was on baggage guard. We left our last encamping ground at 3 A.M. on the 25th; we had only four miles to the Pass, and the Pass was five more, when we reached our new ground, so it was not more than nine miles altogether, yet it was 10 o'clock at night before the rear-guard, bringing up the fag end of the baggage, came in. For nearly the whole of this day I was exposed to an infernally hot sun, and the stench arising from the dead cattle was really frightful. I was also literally twenty-six hours without getting a morsel to eat or a drop to drink, and but the day before on the sick-list. No wonder I was laid up! This Ghwozhe Pass was a great deal worse than any part of the Bolan. It was nothing but a succession of the most difficult ascents and precipitous descents; the most trying kind of ground for the poor camels, who fell down in great numbers, and in some parts the path lay between two high rocks, and was only four feet wide; how the artillery got over it I cannot imagine. A handful of determined men could, I should think, defend it against an army. We were on the *qui vive* the whole time, expecting an attack on the baggage, but we only lost a few camels. Here we caught up the 17th and artillery, which left Dadur before us. If our toils had been great, those of the 17th and artillery were twice as much, as it took them two days and two nights to get the guns through, and they were obliged to bivouack in the Pass, and were attacked once or twice by the Ghiljees, whom, however, one section or so easily drove off. I must now tell you that on leaving the Bolan Pass the Kaukers &c. made their bows to us, but handed us at the same time over to the care of their intimate friends the Ghiljees. These are a kind of half-civilized robbers, a large clan, and abound throughout the whole of Afghanistan. Their chief is a friend of Dost Mahomed. They gave us a little annoyance on the road, but whenever they did so they managed to get the worst of it. They murdered a few poor camp followers. At one place they fired on some grass-cutters belonging to the 4th Light Dragoons, after coming among them and talking with them in a friendly manner, as is their usual custom, in order to ascertain what might be the chance of an attack. A troop of that corps was immediately sent out, with nearly all the officers. Some villagers who had been bringing things to our camp joined the robbers, but the 4th played the d—l with them, killing or wounding about forty, and only one horse belonging to the 4th was wounded. Major Daly, who commands the corps, killed four men himself with a simple bamboo hunting spear, used for killing boars. Sir J. Keane had fourteen of them shot that had been caught stealing camels at Quittah, one march from Siriab, where we left our sick: a brigade of the Bengal army is quartered there.

Well; in spite of Ghiljees, Kaukers, Passes, &c., we reached Candahar on the 4th of May, having only halted two days since we left Dadur,—pretty good work! We were very much disappointed in the country, which is little better than a desert, and the weather cruelly hot. I remember very little of what occurred after I was on the sick-list, except that on arriving at our ground at one place, after a march of eighteen miles, we found that the natives had destroyed the well which was to have supplied us with water,—pleasant news for a man laid up with fever; in consequence of which they made a good profit by bringing it in for sale. About as much as would fill two moderate-sized pitchers was sold for half a rupee, about 14*d.* My European servant came and begged to be allowed to drink the water in my basin with which I had just washed myself, and before I could say anything, drank down the whole of it with a zest as if it had been champagne.

We reached Candahar on the 4th, and on the 8th his Majesty Shah Shooja-ool-Moolk was crowned, after which there was a review of all the troops that were here by his Majesty, a grand "tomasha;" but such, I am told, was the unpopularity of the Shah that out of the whole population of Candahar very few persons were looking on, though the Easterns are devoted sight-hunters. On the — he held a levee, where every officer had the honour of making his leg to his Majesty. I was not present at either of these grand occasions, being at the time still on the sick-list. I, however, had a glimpse of his Majesty the other morning as he was taking his airing. He is a fine-looking man, with a splendid black beard. I am told that he is a very accomplished man, but an exceedingly bad ruler. He has written his own life, which is said to be very interesting: I should think it must be so, as few men have experienced so many changes of fortune as he has. You will find a very good description of him, as well as of Cabool and Sinde, in "Burnes' Travels in Bokhara," the present Sir Alexander Burnes, who is second in command to Macnaghten, and a great deal with the Shah. I read also an excellent article on this country &c. in the last December or January number of "Blackwood's Magazine."

Another horrible murder, somewhat similar to that of Capt. Hand, occurred here about the middle of last month. Two officers of the 16th Lancers, Inverarity and Wilmer, went one day on a fishing excursion to a small river about seven miles from this; several parties had been there before on pic-nic excursions, as it was much cooler, and there were some beautiful gardens, with lots of fruit, on the banks of the stream. There is a slight hill to be crossed in getting to it, at the top of which is a cut-throat narrow pass, formed out of the rock; you must pass through it in single file, and the bottom being of rock is so slippery and rough that it is with difficulty a horse can keep his footing on it. They were returning home about half-past eight o'clock, when Wilmer, being rather wrong in his stomach, got off his horse for a short time, and Inverarity said he would walk to the top of the hill to look at the view by moonlight; Wilmer followed in a few minutes on foot, his ghorewalla following with his horse. On coming near the top of the hill before mentioned, he was somewhat astonished at a large stone whizzing by his head, and immediately afterwards about six or seven men jumped on him out of the rocks. He had time to draw back, and received two different cuts on his walking stick, which cut it through, and slightly wounded him on the forehead. He managed to draw back from another, which was made at him with such strength that the fellow fell with the force of his own blow. Wilmer then thought it was time to cut and run, and bolted as fast as he could with these chaps after him. They luckily, however, stopped to rob his and Inverarity's bangies, containing their kit, which they met his servant carrying, &c. Wilmer did not stop till he reached a detachment of the Shah's force which is stationed there; he returned with a party from them, and on reaching the other side of the hill found poor Inverarity lying on the ground dreadfully mutilated; he was not quite dead when they came up, and Wilmer says he can never forget the convulsive shudder he gave on their arrival, taking them for the murderers returning to finish him. He died, however, almost immediately, merely saying, "For God's sake, look at my hands! I am afraid I am very badly wounded." Thus fell another victim, as we all feel, to the conciliation principle! Neither Inverarity's horse nor anything of their kit has been since seen, though Wilmer has recovered his horse. This will give you a pretty idea of the country we are living in. The next day there was an order out from Sir J. Keane, in which, after giving an account of the murder, he begged all officers never to go out into the country on sporting expeditions unless in large parties and well armed. The Shah and Sir John were also on the point of burning down the village near which the murder occurred, but the political department would not allow it. Seven or eight men were, however, taken up, though nothing certain has been proved. They are still in chains in the town; what will be done with them I don't know. I always have my holster pipes, and pistols loaded, whenever I ride out, as there is nothing like being prepared.

I have little to say of Candahar, which appears to me to be just the same as every other town I have seen in the East, very dirty, &c. It stands in a tolerably fertile plain, with hills scattered all round it. It is a perfect square, each side of which is nearly a mile in length; two streets, one from north to south, the other from east to west, run through it, and bisect each other in the centre: in these are the different bazaars. The rest of the town, as it appeared to me as I rode round the walls the other day, is perfectly deserted. There are double walls to the town, entire all the way round, but I should think it could be easily taken. A great number of the inhabitants have left it on account of the dearness of provisions, occasioned by the hungry mouths of so large a force as ours, and also because, on his first arrival, the Shah wished to play some of his old arbitrary acts over again.

The Ghiljees have been at their old tricks lately, robbing some supplies for the army, which came up by the Bolan Pass about a week ago, and which they followed nearly into our camp. The caravan, however, was under the charge of a right sort of fellow, the Rajah of Buhawulpoor, who was bringing up a contingent to the Shah's force, and if any of his camels were taken away he took two for one from the first village he arrived at. The Ghiljees got more bold afterwards, and actually endeavoured to walk off with the camels of the Bengal army, and five or six were taken prisoners by some Sepoys, and one blown from a gun in the town. They, however, killed one, and severely wounded two other unarmed soldiers of H. M. 13th Light Infantry, who were out with the camels of their regiment, the guard for the camels having very quietly gone to sleep in a house. The poor fellows made a desperate fight, defending themselves with their shoes; and one of them pulled a mounted Ghiljee off his horse, but had his arm cut through before he could get the fellow's sword from him: they lost a great many camels.

June 29th.—Well, to-morrow we are off for Cabool; I hope the country may improve as we advance. Everybody speaks very highly of Cabool itself—a fine climate, 6000 feet above the sea. It has been very hot the whole time we have been here. They say there is plenty of grain to be had on the road; I hope this may be true, and that we shall not have a repetition of what took place before in regard to expense. I was congratulating myself, a day or two since, on the prospect of getting my back pay, but now I hear that I shall not only be minus that, but that we are not to get any more pay for three months, owing to some mismanagement or other; consequently, we shall be obliged to get into debt, with a nice little interest to pay off. I wish, therefore, that next year you would give me credit for another 60*l.* I do not wish you to send it out to me, but that you would let me draw upon you as far as that sum, in case I should find it necessary, as this campaign has sadly crippled me. Your last 60*l.* is nearly gone, and yet I have not spent a farthing that I could help: this irregular way of paying troops is very disgusting to them.

The report is now that we are not likely to have any regular fighting, as it is pretty generally believed that Dost Mahomed has agreed to our terms; the "on dit" is, that he is at Peshawur, and awaits our arrival in Cabool, to give himself up to the British government. Colonel Wade, one of the political diplomatic line, is near Peshawur with a part of Runjet's army, but Dost Mahomed will not surrender himself to him, nor will Colonel Wade cross the Punjab frontiers, on account of the great enmity which exists between the Afghans and Sikhs: however, all this is to be proved. I wish we could have one good brush with them, as we should then have plain sailing; as it is, I suppose we shall be annoyed by these rascally Ghiljees all the way up: out-lying pickets to take care of camels, &c. With regard to the climate of this country I can say little, as we have only been here during the hot weather, and hot we have found it with a vengeance; but then we have been living in tents. One man of ours has died by a coup de soleil; he was one of the camel guard. I do not consider the climate an unhealthy one. It is a very lucky thing for us that we were not left in Sinde: the troops left there have suffered terribly. Sinde is one of the hottest places in the world, and very unhealthy; in fact, I consider it to be about one of the most disgusting countries in the world. The 17th regiment lost an officer there under very melancholy circumstances. He was coming up to join his regiment, having been only lately appointed to it, and lost his way in that dreadful desert I told you of, where he wandered in a wretched state for two days, during which time the simoom came on, and he died from its effects a short time after reaching his tent; the simoom was still so violent that his servants were obliged to dig his grave inside his tent: his body turned black immediately after death.

We have had excellent European fruit here, and the gardens about the place are very large and beautiful—peaches, apricots, cherries, apples, grapes, and mulberries. I never tasted anything more delicious than the melons here. You cannot imagine, in your temperate climate, how refreshing they are on a hot day; but, then, they are said to be very dangerous. The vegetables, too, are good, particularly to those who had been without them so long as we had. There are peas, beans, salad, cucumber, but, unfortunately, no potatoes; what would we not give for a nice mealy murphy! we have not tasted one for four months; however, in all these respects Cabool is much superior. What we shall do when we reach that place I cannot imagine,—one thing, the Hindoo Koosh, prevents our marching further. The report is, that if everything goes smooth we shall go back again this year;

but this I do not believe, as I hardly think it probable that the government would be at such expense in marching us such a distance just to keep us at Cabool for a month, and if we overstay that it will be too late, and the snow and severity of the climate will hinder our returning. Moreover, Runjet Sing is very ill, and, they say, is likely to kick, in which case there will, I take it, be a regular shindy in the Punjab; and John Company, when he has once put his foot into a country, does not withdraw it very soon. Besides, there is Herat and Persia to be looked to. For my part, I have no objection to a winter in Cabool; and if we can only get up our supplies in the liquor line, we shall, I have no doubt, make ourselves very comfortable. The 16th Lancers have an excellent pack of foxhounds with them, and horses are very cheap. There are to be races &c. on a grand scale also when we get there; and if we can get our supplies up by that time, we may look forward to spending a merry Christmas even in such a distant country. How curious all this must sound to you in your quiet, lovely home of Brookhill. I have often thought of you all during this campaign, particularly the other day, when I had the fever; and I hope and trust my life may be spared that I may see you all once more, particularly as I have never seen you at Brookhill.

With regard to myself, my health, with the exception of the fever, has been much better than I could have expected, considering what we have gone through. I have, however, been sadly bothered the whole time

I have been in the country with rheumatism; at times, during the march, I was so bad with it that I could not walk ten minutes at a time. I have also had terrible pains in the joints of my arms, and have them still, and it is with difficulty I can get a gun to my shoulder. I can walk pretty well now, but running is totally out of the question; so that I am afraid I should come off poorly in a hand-to-hand encounter with these rascals. I applied to the doctor for some medicine, but he said "he could give me none;" in fact, they will not give an officer any medicine now unless he is very seriously ill, as they are very short of medical stores.

I hope you may be able to get through this letter; the blue paper I have been writing on is Russian, and bought in Candahar. I do not think I have anything more to say. I will write again when I reach Cabool. Tell Kate I will write to her too: I hope she got my letter which I wrote in January last under cover to you.

With best love to all at home,

Believe me your very affectionate son,

T. W. E. HOLDSWORTH.

P.S.—By-the-bye, there is an officer here in H. M. 13th Light Infantry, with the Bengal force, who knows Arthur very well, in fact, I think a great deal better than I do myself. His name is Wood; he is a Canterbury man, and seems to know Mr. Baylay and everybody else there. He was in the 48th when Arthur was at Canterbury with the 4th Drag. Guards. He desired to be kindly remembered to Arthur when I wrote. I hope Eliza's hooping-cough is well. I was very sorry to hear of poor Sluman's death: as far back as I can recollect he is always associated in my mind with home. I hope Ghiljee, Kauker, Beloochee, and Co., will let this pass.

LETTER VIII.

Camp, near Ghuzni, July 24th, 1839.

MY DEAR FATHER,—You must put down yesterday, the 23rd of July, in your memorandum book as a memorable day for your son Tom, and, I may say, for the British army. Ghuzni, the strongest fortress in Afghanistan, was taken by assault in three-quarters of an hour, by the four European regiments of the army—viz., the Queen's, 13th Light Infantry, 17th regiment, and Bengal European regiment. The storming party, or forlorn hope, consisted of the Light Companies of the four regiments. The whole right in front—ergo, our company (the Light Company of the Queen's) was the first in. I may well remember it, as it was the first time I smelt gunpowder and saw blows given in real earnest. It is the most splendid thing for us that could have happened: if we had failed, we should have had the whole country down upon us in a few days; now, they say, the country is ours.

It is reported that Sir J. Keane was so very anxious about it, that when he heard our first cheers, after entering the gate of the town, he actually cried, it was such a relief to his mind; and that he told Brigadier Sale, lieutenant-colonel of the 13th Light Infantry, who commanded on the occasion, that it was very likely that the fate of India depended on our taking this place. Ghuzni was considered Dost Mahomed's principal fortress; his son commanded in it, and it was garrisoned by 3000 Afghans. Young Dost expected to hold it out for a fortnight; and his father was to have come to his relief in a day or two, when we should have had a difficult part to perform, as we should have been surrounded in this valley by armed parties on all sides; so that it would have been really a ticklish job. They had collected provisions in the town for three months, and arms and ammunition; in fact, it was the regular depôt for their army. They had also about four or five lacs of rupees; but that will not give us much prize money. Our loss was very trifling, owing to the daring and sudden nature of the attack, as they were taken totally by surprise. Our regiment suffered the most, and we have thirty-seven killed and wounded, including officers, of whom six out of eighteen were wounded—one-third of the whole,—however, none of the latter dangerously, thank God, though two of them are returned severely wounded. Five men of our regiment were killed outright on the spot, and I am afraid we shall lose some more in a few days from the effects of their wounds. Of the enemy, about 500 were killed, and more than 1500 made prisoners; and of the remainder, who made their escape over the walls, the greater part were cut down by the Dragoons, or spifflicated by the Lancers. Among the prisoners is young Dost himself, the greatest prize of all. More than a thousand magnificent horses have also been taken, besides pack-horses, camels, and grain in abundance. However, I never can tell a story without going back to the very commencement.

I finished my last letter to you the day before we left Candahar. Well; we started on Sunday, the 30th of June, and made seven marches to Belanti Ghiljee, where we caught up the Shah's army, with a Bengal division. Here Sir John Keane had first come in sight of young Dost's army, who, however, retired very quickly, though there was some talk of their holding out at this place, and we were pushed on rapidly in consequence. They shewed their sense in not holding out there, as it would not have taken us long to dislodge them. We halted here a day, and then marched on by very short and easy marches, halting every third or fourth day, and taking things very easy, although we were constantly annoyed by the Ghiljees, who murdered several of our camp followers, and tried to rob us whenever they could find an opportunity, until we were within five good marches of Ghuzni, when General Willshire received an order to push on by forced marches, and to make these five into three. After making two out of these three, (and precious long ones they were,) we found out that we were still upwards of twenty miles from Ghuzni, with the men so fatigued that it was nearly impossible for them to do it, and that we should therefore be obliged to make two of it. The event, however, proved the contrary; for, about seven o'clock in the evening, a dispatch came from General Willshire, and about eight, just as we were preparing to turn in, the orders were out to strike our tents, and march in an hour's time, and catch up Sir John Keane and the Shah, who were halted about nine miles in advance of us. Sir John was anxious to have the whole force concentrated before marching on Ghuzni. Nothing, however, was certain; and we were all in a high state of excitement, not knowing what to expect: this was the evening of the 20th. We made quick work of this march, and reached Sir John Keane about half-past twelve. Here we heard that Sir John Keane was in expectation of a night attack. He had fallen in that morning with the advance of the enemy, who had, however, upon the appearance of the British force, retired upon Ghuzni. We bivouacked on our ground, after throwing out strong pickets, and marched again at 5 A. M., Sir John Keane, the Bengalees, and cavalry in advance, then the Shah, and then our small party. We, however, sent our artillery to join Sir John. About eight o'clock, when within about three miles of Ghuzni, we heard the first symptoms that the game of war was beginning: our batteries were firing on the place, and the garrison were returning it with good effect; it served as a sort of overture to the opera in which we knew we must soon be actors.

In consequence of the great quantity of baggage, now the whole army was joined, we were halted for a couple of hours to protect it, and the whole of the cavalry was sent back for that purpose; and well it was that they were, as a part of the enemy's cavalry made a demonstration for attacking it, but withdrew on seeing ours. We were at length marched on, and took up our ground a little to the S.W. of the fort, but out of harm's way, when we heard a more definite account of what had been done. The advance of the Bengal column, H. M. 13th Light Infantry and the 16th Native Infantry, had some little work in driving the enemy out of the gardens and old buildings that surround the town. This, however, they accomplished with a trifling loss; our guns then opened on the place, but as they were light ones (the heaviest being still in the rear), with little effect. This desultory fire on both sides was, however, kept up for about three hours: little execution being done, and a few casualties having occurred among the artillery, Sir John Keane ordered the guns to be withdrawn. We had not been on our ground more than three hours when we were ordered once more on the march, and to march by a circuitous route across the mountains, in order to avoid the fire of the town, and take up our ground on the other side of it. We reached our new ground about nine, after a fatiguing march of seven miles, crossing the river, and, by an infernal path, through the hills. Here we bivouacked again for the night, as little of our baggage had arrived.

The enemy took this move of ours as a defeat, and concluded that we had marched on to Cabool, despairing of taking their fort: the event proved how wofully they were mistaken! They wasted a good deal of powder in firing for joy, and young Dost sent a dispatch from the place to his father, apprizing him of the fact, and begging him to come down upon us immediately, while he would follow upon our rear. He also sent to a Ghiljee chieftain near us, telling him to collect as many followers and country people as he could to make an attack upon our baggage, as he had only to come down and take it. We sold this fellow a bargain, however, the next day. Well; the first thing we heard the next morning was from young Keane, and to this effect, that we were to rest for that day, and that the four European corps were to storm the place the next morning before daylight, as the state of the country was such that Sir John could not waste time in breaching it; and, moreover, it was doubtful whether, from the nature of the walls, it could be breached at all. We did not, however, learn the final dispositions till the evening.

That day, the 22nd, I shall never forget; it was a very dismal one; much more so than the next. There was a nervous irritability and excitement about us the whole day; constantly looking at the place through spy-glasses, &c.; and then fellows began to make their wills, and tell each other what they wished to have done in case they fell; altogether it was not at all pleasant, and every one longed most heartily for the morrow, and to have it over. I felt as I used to do when I was a child, and knew I must take a black dose or have a tooth drawn the next morning. About twelve o'clock a great deal of firing took place on our left; this we soon ascertained to be the Ghiljee chief I have before mentioned, coming down with the amiable purpose of lootzing our camp. A part of the Shah's Afghan cavalry, a few guns of the Horse Artillery, and a squadron of Lancers, were ordered out, who soon sent them to the right-about. The chief, when he saw that it was not such an easy job as he expected, cut his stick the first, with his horsemen, about 2000, leaving the poor foot-pads, about 1000, to shift for themselves. They were terribly mauled, and a great number of prisoners taken, whose heads the Shah struck off immediately. Well; evening came at last! and then we heard the morning's news confirmed; that the Light Companies of the four corps were to form the storming party, that an Engineer officer, with some Sappers, each carrying a bag of gunpowder (in all 300lbs.), was to advance to the Cabool gate, and place it there, in order to blow it down; that immediately upon the gates falling we were to rush in and take possession of the town, &c. At the same time a false attack was to be made by the 16th Bengal Native Infantry on the Candahar gate, in order to divert the enemy's attention. Brigadier Sale, lieut.-colonel of the 13th, was to command the whole, and Col. Dennie, of the same corps, the storming party. Three regiments of Native Infantry were to be in reserve, under Sir Willoughby Cotton; and the cavalry were to be stationed so as best to intercept the flight of those who might manage to make their escape from the place. We were to be formed ready for the attack at two o'clock in the morning, close to a high pillar, about half a mile from the fort; we were to advance under cover of the Artillery, who were to fire over and clear the walls for us. I laid down in my cloak directly after mess, and, being dreadfully tired, never slept more soundly than I did the night before the storming of Ghuzni.

At one o'clock we turned out; I took a cup of tea and a couple of ginger biscuits, and joined my company: in a quarter of an hour we were on our march to the pillar, where we were to be formed. Here we found Col. Sale and the Engineer officers, &c. Col. Sale called out the officers, and told them the plan of the attack, which was to be the same as mentioned before, except that the 13th Light Infantry were to line the ditch outside the town, and fire on the ramparts, while we advanced. The storming party, Queen's and Bengal European regiments, were, after entering the gate, to move along a street to the left, clearing the houses, &c., and on arriving at the end to mount the ramparts, and to return by them. Our object in doing this was to drive as many men as possible into the citadel, and having obtained this object, a signal was to be given, and the artillery were to fire shells into the citadel, which, particularly as their powder magazine was there, it was expected would soon make them cut and run. The 17th and 13th regiments being nearest, were then to rush up and take possession of the citadel, and the Native regiments, being in reserve, were to assist them. Col. Sale then said a few words of encouragement, and concluded by hoping "we should all have luck"—on the whole a very neat and appropriate speech. We then piled arms, and officers fell out. I never saw fellows more merry than most of us were while we were waiting there; in fact, if we had been going to the most delightful place in the world, we could not have appeared in better spirits; and this put me strongly in mind of a scene I had read in a book called "The Subaltern," where the feelings of the officers, waiting for an attack, are described as being just the same. At length, "bang" went a gun from our batteries. Col. Sale said, "Ah, there goes the signal; we had better be starting:" just as if one was to get ready to take a ride to Brixham or elsewhere. Well; we fell in, and in about a quarter of an hour off we went. The enemy returned the fire from our batteries in good style, and there was a regular row. They pointed their "Long Tom," a fifty-two pounder, towards us, and sent the shot over our heads and a little to our left. The ball made a terrific row rushing over us. Whilst we were marching down to the attack the fire on both sides was at its height. The noise was fearful, and the whole scene the grandest and, at the same time, the most awful I ever witnessed. I caught myself, once or twice, trying to make myself as small as I could. As we got nearer the gate it grew worse, and the enemy, from their loop-holes, began to pepper us with matchlocks and arrows. The scene now was splendid. The enemy, at the commencement of the firing, threw out blue lights in several places, which looked beautiful, and the flames of their and our artillery, together with the smaller flashes from the matchlock men, added to the roar of their big guns, the sharp cracking of the matchlocks, the whizzing of their cannon balls and ours, (the latter of which, by-the-bye, went much nearer our heads than the enemy's, as our artillery fired beautifully, and sent their shot close over our heads, on the ramparts,) the singing of the bullets, and the whizzing of their arrows, all combined, made up as pretty a little row as one would wish to hear. Add to this, that it was as dark as pitch, and you may judge of the effect. We made a rush over the bridge, which the enemy had not destroyed, and continuing it up a slight ascent, we found ourselves of a sudden close to the gate. Here there was a check. Although the gate was blown down, still the remains of it, and the barricade on the inside, rendered it a difficult place to get over, particularly as it wanted at least half an hour of daylight, and was perfectly dark. The two first sections were therefore a long time getting through, during which the two last, to which I belonged, were standing still outside, exposed to a cross fire from two round towers, which flanked the entrance. Our men, however, kept up such a smart fire upon every hole and opening that no man dared shew his nose, and their fire was therefore rendered harmless. At length we moved in, and found that, besides what I have mentioned above, there was a large hole in the roof of the portico over the gate, through which the enemy were pitching earth, beams of wood, stones, &c.; one of these beams knocked over my European servant, who was next to me, and dislocated his arm, and, taking me in the flank, made me bite the dust also; however, I had no further hurt than a slight bruise, and was up again immediately, as I heard one of the soldiers say, "Oh! there is poor Mr. Holdsworth: he's down!"

On getting within the gate a few volleys cleared the opening of the street. Robinson, (our captain,) Col.

Sale, with Kershaw and Wood of the 13th, Sale's staff, (the latter the man who knew Arthur at Canterbury,) were the first in. Poor Col. Sale got a cut in the mouth, and fell upon Kershaw, who went down with him; on rising, an Afghan was lifting his sword to cut down Sale, when Kershaw seized the hilt of his sword, and ran his own into him. Robinson also got a terrible cut on the side of his head, which would have done his business for him if he had not had on a cap padded with cotton, which deadened the weight of the blow. All the companies of the storming party, however, got in well, except the last, the light company of the Bengal European regiment, and they had a desperate fight, the enemy having returned to the gate in great numbers, and twenty-seven men of the company were laid low in no time. After this every company that came in had a shindy at the gate; the fact was, that the enemy took every company for the last, and therefore made a desperate attempt to escape through it. Our company, with the advance, pushed through the town, clearing the tops of the houses. We only lost one man of our company; we thought he was done for at first, but he is still alive, and, I am glad to say, likely to do well; he was shot right through the breastplate, and the ball went round his body and was taken out of his back; he is to wear the same breastplate in future. On coming to the end of the town we halted, and were agreeably surprised, shortly after, to see the British flag waving on the top of the citadel:

the fact of the matter was, that the enemy never thought of retiring to the citadel at all, but endeavoured to make their escape directly they found we were inside the gates; the 17th and 13th, therefore, quietly marched up and took possession of it.

We now returned by the ramparts, taking a great number of prisoners, and on reaching the large street where the horses were, the scene was perfectly ridiculous; the horses were loose, and running and charging about in all directions, kicking, fighting, &c. On getting near the gate we entered by, the effects of our fight became more apparent, as dying and dead Afghans testified. There were eight lying at one particular spot, where a tumbril had blown up, and their bodies were still burning from the effects. I never saw finer men than some of these Afghans—they were perfect models. The plunder now began, though to little purpose, as prize agents were at the gates and made most of us refund. I managed, however, to get through a rather handsome spear, which I took from before the tent of one of the chiefs. If the carelessness of my servants will allow it I mean to keep it till we get back, whenever that may be, and send it home by some trusty person, when perhaps you may think it worthy of a place among your curiosities at Brookhill. The 13th and 17th, however, had the best of it in the citadel, which was also the palace, and where all young Dost's women were. I hear that the soldiers have possession of some very handsome articles which they boned there I believe. After this, young Dost, or, to give him his right name, Hyder Khan, was found in a large hole near the citadel, with about twenty followers; they had some work, however, in securing him. About this time I saw the Shah, with the diplomatic people, Sir J. Keane, and Sir W. Cotton, enter the fort and proceed to the citadel. The old Shah was mightily delighted, as well he might be, and expressed himself in raptures with the European soldiery. I was back again to breakfast at mess by eight o'clock. Several of our men were wounded by arrows. One soldier swore "that a fellow had shot his ramrod into him." Stisted had an arrow through the calf of his leg, but his wound is not considered of any importance.

July 30*th*.—Sir J. Keane, with the greater part of the army, marched this morning for Cabool; ours (the Bombay division) march to-morrow. Although the greater part of the town was taken in the way I have described, still a party of about 100 men, under Dost Mahomed's standard-bearer, (a great man, of course,) held out till the next day, when they were all taken, and soon afterwards shot. They certainly must have been assisted by some Europeans, as their powder was made up in a very scientific manner, and their grape was exceedingly well put together. Young Dost cannot imagine how the gate was blown down; he thinks, I hear, that we shot two men inside the fort from a big gun, who opened the door for us. He was sleeping over it at the time; the explosion must have "astonished him a few, I guess." He says some of his father's best soldiers have fallen there; and one man in particular, a great chief, said to be the best swordsman between Cabool and Candahar. I have been in the fort since, and I am glad we took it in the dark, as it is not at all a nice looking place by daylight. The rooms in the citadel are very fine, particularly where the women were, the ceilings of which are inlaid with gold work. All our sick and wounded are to be left here: we only leave one officer behind, poor Young, who was shot through the thigh very near the groin.

Reports have been very various since the fall of Ghuzni whether Dost himself will fight or not. It seems to be generally expected that we shall have another shindy before we get to Cabool, though a great number of chiefs have lately come in to the Shah, among the principal of whom is Hadjee Khan Kauker, the governor of Bamian, a man of great influence in the country, and a great intriguer, formerly a great friend of Dost Mahomed's. He came in to us about three hours after the place had fallen: he had been waiting on the top of a hill to see the result, and was prepared to join whichever side was victorious. I must tell you, also, that on the 21st, the day we marched upon Ghuzni, another son of Dost was waiting outside the town to attack us with about three thousand men; but on seeing the size of our army he thought better of it, and cut for Cabool as fast as he could; he was deserted on the way by most of his army, and reached Cabool with scarcely a follower: his father was exceedingly enraged, and is said to have put him in prison.

Sunday, 28th. — The day before yesterday, Dost Mahomed's brother, a man who has always favoured the English, and advised Dost to have nothing to do with the Persians, &c., but who lives quite retired, and has very little to do with politics, came into our camp to endeavour to make terms for his brother; but, it is said, neither party was satisfied: they say that he was disgusted at our proposals, and replied, "that Dost would rather lose his life than accept them." Dost wants to be made the Shah's vizier; but that, of course, could not be allowed. How it will end no one knows: however, a few days will shew. We have had several deserters from Dost's army; they say he is encamped, and has thrown up strong entrenchments about three miles in front of Cabool. I should hardly, however, think that the people of Cabool will allow his doing so, as there are several rich people in it who would not like to see Ghuzni reacted at their own door. There would be lots of prize money for us. Talking of prize money, I am afraid there will not be very much, though the things that were taken sold remarkably well, as did also the horses, &c. I managed to buy, though for much beyond its value, a rather pretty coverlet for a bed, which was taken in the fort, which perhaps belonged to some of the young ladies of the harem; it is of shawl velvet, and said to be made in Cashmere. I intend to send it home with the spear, and give it to Kate; though what use she can put it to I hardly know, as I am sure it will not be large enough for her bed; still, when one considers whence it was taken, it may possess some little interest. Young Dost is left behind in the fort, which is to be strongly garrisoned, and where we leave all our sick and wounded.

The climate of this place is delightful; it is about 6000 feet above the level of the sea; and although this is the hottest month in the year, still we do not find it at all unpleasant, living in tents: a delightful change from Candahar. There is the most beautiful clover here I ever saw, and lots of fruit.

We have just received intelligence of Runjet Sing's death; he has been reported dead several times before; but they say this time it is really the case; if so, we are still only at the beginning of our work, as we shall most likely have something to do in the Punjab. The government, it is said, have guaranteed the succession of Runjet's son, who is little better than a natural idiot. The chiefs of the Sikhs, who are very warlike people, and have often licked the Afghans, say they will not consent to be ruled by such a person, —thereon hangs the matter. A large force has been gradually concentrating at Delhi, Meerut, Loodiana, and all the north-west stations in Bengal, ready to march into the Punjab in case of Runjet's death, which has been long expected; and we very likely shall make an advance by the line of the Cabool river to Peshawur, and Attock, on the Indus. It is rather late to begin a campaign after marching more than a thousand miles, and not meeting an enemy except robbers. If I ever do get home safe and sound after all this work, I shall consider myself very lucky.

July 31*st.*—Here we are, our first day's march to Cabool. Reports still flying about as to whether Dost means to fight. I wore the pistols you gave me in London at the storming,—they are a capital pair! The post goes directly, so I must conclude, with best love to all, your very affectionate son,

T. W. E. HOLDSWORTH.

P.S. — They say Shah Shooja will give us all medals when everything is settled; those for the officers to be a small gold one, with an impression of the Fort of Ghuzni; those for the soldiers to be silver, and the same pattern. If you look into the military papers when this reaches you, I dare say you will find further accounts of the business.

NOTE.—" It was arranged that an explosion party, consisting of three officers of engineers (Capt. Peat, Lieuts. Durand and M'Leod), three serjeants and eighteen men of the sappers in working dresses, carrying three hundred pounds of powder in twelve sand bags, with a hose seventy-two feet long, should be ready to move down to the gateway at break of day.

" So quickly was the operation performed, and so little was the enemy aware of the nature of it, that not a man of the party was hurt."—*From Memoranda of Capt. Thompson, R.E., Chief Engineer, Army of Indus.*

LETTER IX.

MEMORANDUM.—I have lost this letter, which I regret the more, because it gave a very full account both of Cabool and its environs, as well as of many interesting circumstances which took place during the time the Bombay division of the army remained there.

As far as I remember its contents, it began with the march of the army from Ghuzni to Cabool, the desertion of the troops of Dost Mahomed, and his flight from the capital. It described his pursuit by a party of officers and cavalry, volunteers from the British army, commanded by Captain Outram, who accompanied Hadjee Khan Kauker, the principal chief of the country, with a body of 2000 Afghans, who had joined Shah Shooja at Ghuzni.

It stated, that after a few days had expired, the party had nearly reached the fugitive, when Hadjee Khan refused to proceed, stating, amongst other excuses, that his men had dispersed to plunder, and that he had not any means of preventing it; and Captain Outram was obliged to proceed without him. It had been supposed by Shah Shooja, that Hadjee Khan had been so committed with Dost Mahomed that he might be safely trusted upon this occasion; but there is not the least doubt but that he was engaged in correspondence with him during the whole time, and that Dost Mahomed was thus enabled to effect his escape with his family, although Captain Outram with his party pursued him as far as Bamian. If Hadjee Khan had not acted in this most treacherous way, there could not be a doubt but that Dost Mahomed must have fallen into the hands of Captain Outram. Thus Hadjee Khan proved his double treachery; for which, on his return to Cabool, it was understood the Shah would have put him to death, but for the presence of the English, upon whose interference his sentence was changed to perpetual confinement in one of the state prisons.

It described, also, the arrival of the eldest son of Shah Shooja, with the contingent from Runjet Sing; his meeting with his youngest brother on the road, near the city, who went out for that purpose upon an elephant, richly caparisoned, attended by a suitable cortège; his reception by the British army, and afterwards by his father, at the Bala Hissar, where my son mixed with the troops of the Shah, who filled the palace yard, and was thus enabled to witness the first interview, which was anything but that which might have been expected when the eldest son arrived at the palace to congratulate his father on his restoration to his throne. The King was seated alone in an open balcony, slightly raised above the court, where his officers of state were ranged on either side, on the ground. The Prince advanced through a line of troops and public officers, but did not raise his eyes from the ground. When he came near his father, he prostrated himself in submission to the King, who called to him "that he was welcome;" after which the son ascended to the balcony, where he again made a prostration, when his father raised him up, and seated him near him. The peculiarly careful conduct of the son on his approach appears to have arisen from a consciousness of his father's jealous and suspicious temper, and a fear lest even a smile interchanged with a friend at the court might be construed into hidden treachery. Soon after this, the chief persons of the court made their salutations to the King, to each of whom he said a few words, and the ceremony was ended.

My son added, that he little expected when he was at the levee of his late Majesty King William, before he left England, that the next ceremony of the sort at which he should be present would be that of the King of Afghanistan, in Central Asia, a person with whose name and country he had not then the slightest acquaintance.

The youngest son of Shah Shooja, whom I have mentioned, is described as a beautiful boy, under twelve years of age, ruddy and fair as an English child. He is a great favourite with his father at present, and usually accompanies the Shah wherever he goes. His childhood probably protects him from suspicion of treachery or intrigue.

My son appeared to have mixed occasionally with the inhabitants of Cabool, and, through the introduction of the Persian interpreter, to have become personally acquainted with some of the leading persons of the city. They are described by him as being particularly affable and civil to the officers of our army, with some of whom he paid a visit to a man of rank, at his country-house, and with whom they dined. Nothing could exceed the attention of their host. He shewed them his stud, consisting of more than fifty horses, and every other thing that he possessed, (except his women,) and the hospitality and good fare was unbounded. Neither was the curiosity of these persons less in inquiring minutely into everything they saw when they visited the officers in the camp, than their desire to please in their own houses; and he appeared to have left the place with a most favourable impression of the upper ranks of the city.

Of the city itself, its magnificent bazaar, filled with the richest manufactures of the East, its gardens abounding with the finest fruits in the world, and the fertile country that surrounds it, his description is the same as that which will be found much more at length in the Travels of Lieut. Burnes, in 1832.

Cricket and horse-racing appeared to be the chief recreation of the army during the time it remained inactive; and the two divisions having fortunately come from different Presidencies, the same spirit of rivalry amongst the officers, in the sports of the camp, was as naturally excited at Cabool as in any of the counties or garrisons of their native land.

The evening before they left their ground, two miles from Cabool, he was sent with a subaltern's party to search through all the worst parts of the city for men who were missing from the camp, but after spending many hours, he returned without finding any. They had been paid the day before, and had got away to the liquor-shops; but all turned up in the morning except one, whose body was found murdered, near the camp.

A. H. HOLDSWORTH.

LETTER X.

Camp at Kotree, in Cutch Gundava,
December 8th, 1839.

My dear Father,—As I am now tolerably recovered, and my wounds nearly healed, I take the first opportunity (as my arm is losing its stiffness) of writing to you, as I have no doubt you will be very anxious to hear how I am going on. I desired Stisted, the day after the taking of Kelat, to write, as I was myself then unable. I have no doubt but that he did so; yet I know you must have been anxious before you heard the final result; and I am now happy to inform you that I am getting rapidly well, and expect in a short time to be out of the "sick list." My wound was esteemed a rather ugly one at first; and I must consider it one of the most fortunate cases of Providence that the bullet took the direction it did, as had it swerved in the least degree it must have gone through my lungs, or downward through my liver; and in either case would most likely have done my business completely. As the man who fired at me was so very close, the ball went clear through, and so saved me from the unpleasant process of having it extracted by the doctor, &c. I had my right flank exposed to the man who pinked me, and so the ball passed through my right arm into my right side, and passing downwards to the rear, came out at my back, about an inch from the back-bone. Had it passed to the front instead of to the rear, I should have most assuredly left my bones at Kelat: as it was, from my coughing up a tolerable quantity of blood when I was first hit, the doctor imagined that my lungs had been affected, and for a couple of days, as I have since heard, was very doubtful as to my eventual recovery. However, I may now, I believe, consider myself completely out of the wood.

I find I have not written since the last day I was at Cabool; and I have had few opportunities of doing so, as we have been on the move ever since, and until we reached Kelat there was very little to write about. We broke ground and marched to the other side of Cabool on Monday, the 16th of September, and halted on the 17th for a grand tomasha at the Bala Hissar, or Shah's Palace, being no less than the investiture of the order of the Doorannee Pearl, which was conferred by Shah Shooja on the big-wigs of the army. Sir John Keane, Sir Willoughby Cotton, and Mr. Macnaghten get the first order; generals of divisions and brigadiers, the second; and all field officers engaged at Ghuzni and heads of departments, the third; for the rest, all officers engaged at Ghuzni get a gold medal, and the soldiers a silver one: however, all this depends on the will and sanction of Queen Victoria.

On Wednesday, the 18th, we took our final leave of Cabool and its beautiful environs, and reached Ghuzni on the 26th, where we halted two days, and then struck off in a new direction, straight across country to Quettah, by a new road, and very little known, leaving Candahar to our right, and thereby cutting off a considerable angle. Our object in doing this was, besides saving distance, to afford assistance, if required, to Captain Outram, who had preceded us by about a week, and was gone with some of the Shah's force into the Ghiljee country, and was employed in destroying the forts, &c., of some of the refractory Ghiljee chiefs. He captured one fort, in which were found forty or fifty fellows who were identified as being the same men who had murdered so many camp followers and some of our officers during our march through the country. I saw them at Ghuzni, where they were under confinement, and about to be executed in a few days, as I was told. About eight marches from Ghuzni, Outram sent to General Willshire for assistance, as his force was not sufficient; he was then before the largest of these hill forts, belonging to one of the most influential and refractory of the chiefs, and who had given us a great deal of annoyance in our way up. A wing of the 19th Native Infantry, some Artillery, and the Light Companies were therefore sent to his assistance; but they made a miserable failure, as the chief, putting himself at the head of about a hundred faithful followers, dashed through their pickets at night, and made his escape with all his valuables, and without losing a man. We marched at an easy pace, detaching a force now and then to take a fort, which was invariably found deserted on our approach. Nevertheless, we had hard work of it, as our route lay through and over high and barren mountains, with scarcely an inhabitant or village to be seen, and nothing to be got for our cattle. For three days my horse, and those of most of us, lived on bushes and rank grass that we found occasionally. We had to depend on our commissariat for everything; and they found it difficult to supply grain for the staff and field officers' horses, so, of course, ours were quite left out of the question. Guns, powder, and shot were in great requisition; and, luckily, hares and Khorassan partridges were tolerably abundant. At times, even our guides confessed themselves at fault, so difficult was it to make our way through such a country. However, one thing was greatly in our favour—we had a splendid, bracing climate the whole way, the nights and mornings being "*raything*" too cold, the thermometer ranging at that time between 20 and 30 degrees. The poor Sepoys and camp-followers, however, suffered severely. We experienced scarcely the slightest annoyance from the inhabitants, although we passed through the most disaffected part of the country—viz., the Ghiljee country, and latterly through the heart of the Kauker country, whose chief, Hadjee Khan Kauker, is a prisoner at Cabool, as I told you in my former letter.

At length, on the 31st of October, we reached Quettah, where we were delighted to find a few Parsee merchants, who had come up from Bombay, and from whom we were enabled to get a few European comforts, in the shape of brandy, gin, wine, tea, pickles, &c., which we had long been without; even milk and butter were luxuries to us.

General Willshire now ordered the 31st Bengal Native Infantry, which had been left here in our march up, together with H. M. 17th, and a small detail of Artillery, to proceed to Kelat, under Colonel Baumgardt, our Brigadier. The 31st were to garrison it; and the 17th were sent because Mehrab Khan, the Kelat chief, had declared that "he would not surrender to any but European troops, and see the Sepoys d—d first, if they came alone." However, no resistance was expected, as Mehrab had been offered very liberal terms, which he had apparently accepted. The rest of the force was to go down by the Bolan Pass, and wait at Bukkur, or somewhere in Upper Sinde, till joined by the 17th. However, the next day a new order came out, and the Queen's, together with a stronger detail of Artillery, were ordered to reinforce the detachment to Kelat.

Well; we marched on the 5th of November; and the next day, after we had reached our ground, when we had just sat down to breakfast, great was our surprise to see General Willshire himself ride into camp with a few of his staff. All we could learn on the subject was, that on that morning, which was the day fixed for the rest of the division to begin their march down the Bolan Pass, and just as they were about to start, the General sent for his Adjutant and Quarter-master-general, and, taking them and his Aides with him, started for our camp. Things now looked a little more warlike; still we experienced no annoyance during the whole march; few of us but thought that on our approach Mehrab Khan would give in.

We halted a day at Mostrong, which was about half way, and here General Willshire and the political agent communicated with the Khan, who replied, that "as to the terms, he was willing to meet General Willshire half way, with a small escort, and there talk them over; but that if we advanced against him with an army, he should shut his gates, and we should find him at the door of his citadel with his drawn sword." There was "no mistake about that 'ere," as Sam Weller would say. However, most of us thought it was merely bravado, as our progress was not molested at all; this, however, was afterwards accounted for by the Khan's having called in all his fighting-men to his standard.

The last three days before arriving at Kelat we marched in order of battle, and had strong pickets at night, the whole force sleeping on their arms, and ready to fall in at a moment's notice.

On the 12th we were within eight miles of the fort; and on our arriving on our ground a few horsemen were observed reconnoitring us, who fired on our advance, but retired leisurely on the approach of the column. By that hour the next day "Kelat was prize money." We strongly expected to be attacked that night, and were all ready for a shindy; the artillery loaded with grape, and port-fires lighted, &c. However, it passed over very quietly; but we had hardly marched a mile from our encampment the next morning, when, in an opening through the hill to our right, we observed a large cloud of dust, which we soon discovered to be raised by a strong body of horsemen. They were about a mile and a half from our flank, and kept moving on in a parallel line with our column. However, at a point where the road took a turn towards the hills they halted, at about 150 yards from the advance guard, and deliberately fired into them with their matchlocks, but at too great a distance to do much harm. One company from the advance was sent to dislodge them; upon which they moved quickly down towards the main body, and taking up a position at about the same distance from us as before from the advance, gave us the same salute as they had before treated those in front to. Their balls came whistling in upon us on all sides, and knocked up the dust like drops of rain, but no damage was done; they then galloped off. It was a great pity we had no more cavalry with us; only fifty Bengal, or Irregular Horse, and their cattle were so done up that they were perfectly useless. The enemy laughed at the advance companies that were now sent out to skirmish with them. The ground consisted of undulating hills, and rather rough, over which our skirmishers, encumbered as they were with knapsacks and other absurdities, "selon les regles," found it very difficult to move quickly, and the enemy, riding their sure-footed horses to the top of one of those hills, would fire down, and wheel round, and be under cover of the other side of the hill before our men could return the compliment effectually. If we had had a squadron of Dragoons with us, lightly equipped, the result would have been very different. But, unfortunately, the only time during nearly the whole campaign when cavalry would have been of important service to us we were without them. However, very little blood is ever shed in desultory affairs of this sort, and they only wounded about three or four of our men; and at one place, a party of them coming unexpectedly upon the reserve of the skirmishers, two sections opened a fire upon them, emptied a few saddles, and sent the rest flying. We with the main body had a very good view of the whole affair, and a very animating scene it was. Our road had hitherto lain through a valley, about four miles broad; but when within about three miles and a half from Kelat, it takes a sudden turn to the right, and leads, for the next mile and a half, through a narrow and straight pass, after penetrating which, and arriving at the debouche, the fortress of Kelat appeared before us, frowning defiance. The first sight of it had certainly a very pretty effect: the sun had just burst out, and was lighting the half-cultivated valley beneath us, interspersed with fields, gardens, ruinous mosques, houses, &c.; while Kelat, being under the lee of some high hills, was still in the shade; so that, while all around presented a smiling and inviting appearance, as if hailing our approach with gladness, the fortress above seemed to maintain a dark and gloomy reserve, in high contrast with the rest of the picture; nor was the effect diminished when a thin cloud of smoke was seen spouting forth and curling over its battlements, followed, in a short interval, by the report of a large gun, which came booming over the hills towards us. "Hurrah! they have fired the first shot," was the exclamation of some of us, "and Kelat is prize-money!" On looking more minutely at it, however, it had rather an ugly appearance, and seemed, at that distance, much more formidable than Ghuzni did at the first view. We could only see the citadel, which was much more commanding and difficult of access than that of Ghuzni. The outworks, however, as we afterwards found, were not half so strong; these were, however, hidden from our view by two hills, rather formidable in appearance, covering the approach to the fortress, on each of which a redoubt was erected, and which we could perceive covered with men. Beneath us in the valley the advance companies were seen pushing on to occupy the gardens and other inclosures, while nearer the fort we could observe the body of cavalry we had been before engaged with drawn up, as if waiting our approach, under cover of the redoubts on the hills. Half way down the road leading into the valley was our Artillery, consisting of four six-pounders, field-pieces belonging to the Shah, and two nine-inch howitzers, with our Horse Artillery. Here, also, was General Willshire and staff, who now ordered one of the guns to open on the horsemen, in order to cover the movements of the advance companies, who were driving the enemy's matchlock men before them out of the inclosures in good style. The first shot struck wide of them, the second kicked up a dust rather too close to be pleasant, and the third went slap in among them, knocking over a horse or two, when these gallant cavaliers cut their sticks, and we saw no more of them. We soon moved into the valley, and halted for a considerable time at the foot of the hill. We were here within three-quarters of a mile of the nearest redoubt, and about a mile and half from Kelat itself. General Willshire now made a reconnoissance, and the men from the different baggage guards came in and joined their respective regiments. After halting here about an hour, (the guns from the nearest redoubt every now and then pitching a shot rather close to us,) the brigade-major made his appearance with orders for the three regiments to form in quarter distance column of companies, to attack the two redoubts, each leaving one company with the colours to form the reserve. The 17th were to attack the nearest redoubt, and the 31st Bengal Native Infantry to turn its right, while we were to push on and carry the other, which was the nearest to the fort. At the same time, our artillery were brought into position, and covered our advance.

The plot now began to thicken, and altogether the whole affair was the most exciting thing I ever experienced, and beat Ghuzni out of the pit. We moved steadily on, the guns from the redoubts blazing at us as fast as they could load them; but they were very inferior workmen, and only two shots struck near us, one knocking up the dust close to us, and bounding over our heads, and the other whizzing close over our leading company; however, they kept their ground till we arrived at the foot of the hills, when our artillery having unshipped one of their guns, and otherwise deranged their redoubts, they exploded their powder, and retired, some leisurely, but most in the greatest disorder. Here, again, we had occasion to regret having no cavalry, as a troop or two would have effectually cut off or dispersed them. On reaching the top of the hill which they had abandoned, we found ourselves within a quarter of a mile of the lower end of the town, with the Beloochees making the best of their way towards the gate, which was open to admit them. Captain Outram here rode up to us, and cried out, "On men, and take the gate before they can all get in." This acted like magic on the men. All order was lost, and we rushed madly down the hill on the flying enemy, more like hounds with the chase in view than disciplined soldiers. The consequence was, we were exposed to a most galling fire from the ramparts, by which several of our best men were put *hors de combat;* the fugitives were too quick for us, and suddenly the cry was raised by our leading men, "The gate is shut." All was now the greatest confusion, and shelter was sought for wherever it could be found. Unluckily a rush was made by the greatest part of the regiment to an old shell of a house, which could scarcely afford cover to twenty men, much less to the numbers who thronged into it, and who were so closely jammed that they could not move; and so the outside portion were exposed to the fire from the left bastion of the town, which completely out-flanked them, and from which the matchlock-men kept pouring in a cool and most destructive fire upon this dense mass with the utmost impunity; while a wide, broken-down doorway in the centre exposed them to a fire from another bastion in their front, if ever they shewed their nose for an instant to see how matters were going on, or to return their fire. Poor fellows! you may guess their situation was anything but pleasant. The consequences soon began to shew themselves—eight men and one officer (poor Gravatt) were shot dead, and several more were severely wounded, and had the artillery been less expeditious in knocking down the gate, the greatest part of them would have been annihilated. The other part of the regiment (myself among the rest) were more fortunate. Seeing so many rushing to one place, I made for another shelter, about twenty paces to the rear, which consisted of a long wall, about five feet high, and which afforded ample cover to us all. It was within seventy yards of the bastion that proved so fatal to the other party, and from which they kept up a pretty good fire upon us whenever we exposed ourselves. However, I was so excited that nothing would do but I must see the whole affair; this, however, was rather foolish, as every now and then they would direct their attention to us, and send in a volley, which would sing over us and knock up the dust and the old wall about us in good style. Simmons's horse (the Adjutant's) was foolishly brought down, and had not been a second there when it was shot slap through the hind-leg. The ground behind us was raised a little, so that the horse's leg was in a line with and nearly touching my head as I stood looking over the wall; on reaching the cover we found four or five poor fellows who had been wounded in the rush down the hill, and who had crawled in here as well as they could.

I had an excellent view of the further proceedings from this place. Right above us on the redoubt, from which we had driven the enemy, our artillery had now established themselves, and were slapping away as hard as they could at the gate. I could see every shot as it struck: they made some very clever shots, sending the balls all about the gate, and sometimes knocking down a portion of the bastion over it, considerably deranging the operations of the matchlock-men who were in it; but still the old gate would not fall. In the mean time, the advance companies, which had been in quiet possession of the gardens, inclosures, &c., since the beginning of the affair, were now ordered up to a wall about thirty yards in front of the doorway. They had to run over about three hundred yards of open country before they could get to it, exposed to a fire from the bastion over the door. I saw them make a splendid rush, but three poor fellows and a native water-bearer fell, whom I saw crawl under cover afterwards. All this time the artillery were banging away, but as they made so slight an impression on the gate, two guns of the Shah's were moved down the hill a little to our left, and within about one hundred and fifty yards of the gate. They fired two shots; the first made the old gate shake; the second was more fortunate, and took it about the middle, and brought it completely down. Our men gave a general hurrah; and Outram galloping down the hill at full speed, gave the word, "Forward;" and General Willshire came up to us at his best pace, waving his hat, "Forward, Queen's," he sung out, "or the 17th will be in before you." On we rushed again for the gate as hard as we could; the enemy treated us to one more volley, by which they did some execution, and Dickenson was wounded in his leg, and then abandoning the lower defences of the town, retreated to the citadel.

However, on entering the gate, we found matters not so easy as we expected. The streets were very narrow and so intricate that they formed a perfect labyrinth, and it was very difficult to make any progress through them. The men, therefore, soon got scattered about and broken into small parties; and some, I am afraid, thought of loot, or plunder, more than of endeavouring to find their way to the citadel. I forgot to mention that during the time we were under cover, the 17th and 31st Native Infantry had moved round the hill and taken up a position on our right. These two regiments were ordered forward and into the town and at the same time and the same gate as we were. The whole force, therefore, entered the town nearly together. I followed with a party of our men, and we pushed along as well as we could through streets, by-ways, &c.

This was rather nervous work, as we never could tell what we had to expect before us; there was no open enemy to be seen, but whenever we came to an opening exposed to the citadel, a few bullets invariably came whizzing in about us, and knocked over a man or two; moreover, having the recollection of Ghuzni fresh in our minds, we expected every moment a rush of some desperate fellows from the narrow holes we passed through. After groping my way through narrow passages and all sorts of agreeable places, I found myself in the exact spot I had started from—viz., the gate by which we had entered. Here a man of our Light Company came and told me that he had discovered a way to the citadel, and begged me to put myself at the head of a few men there collected. Of course I did so, and in a short time we found ourselves in a large courtyard, with stables, &c., full of horses and Beloochees, right under the windows of the citadel. These men cried out for "amān," or "mercy;" but the soldiers recollecting the treachery that had been practised at Ghuzni in a similar case were going to shoot the whole kit of them. Not liking to see this done, I stopped their fire, and endeavoured to make the Beloochees come out of their holes and give themselves up. I was standing at this time in the centre of the court, and had heard a few shots whizzing rather close over my head, when I suddenly received a shock, which made me think at the moment I was smashed to bits, by a ball from a ginjall, or native wall piece. I was knocked senseless to the ground, in which state I suppose I lay for a few minutes, and when I came to myself I found myself kicking away, and coughing up globules of clotted blood at a great pace. I thought at first I was as good as done for; however, on regaining a little strength, I looked around, and seeing none of our men in the place, and thinking it more than probable, from what I knew of their character, that the very men whom I had been endeavouring to save might take it into their heads to give me the "*coup de grace*" now I was left alone, I made a desperate effort, got on my legs, and managed to hobble out, when I soon found some of our men, who supported me until a dooly could be brought, into which I was placed, and was soon on my way to the doctor.

You may imagine my feelings all this time to be anything but pleasant. I still continued coughing up blood, which was flowing also pretty freely from my side. The idea that you may probably have only a few hours longer to exist, with the many recollections that crowd into your mind at such a time, is anything but a delightful one; and the being so suddenly reduced from a state of vigorous activity to the sick, faintish feeling that came over me, by no means added to the *agremens* of my situation.

I well recollect being carried through the gate, where General Willshire with his staff and the officers who had been left with the reserve companies were, and who all pressed forward to see who the unfortunate fellow in the dooly was, when the low exclamation of "Poor Holdsworth!" and the mysterious and mournful shaking of heads which passed among them, by no means tended to enliven my spirits. I soon reached the place where the doctors, with their understrappers, were busily employed among the wounded, dying, and dead. I was immediately stripped and examined, and then, for the first time, heard that the ball had passed through and out of my body. I also now discovered that it had struck and gone through my arm as well. Being very anxious, I begged Hunter, the doctor, to let me know the worst. He shook his head, and told me "he thought it a rather dangerous case, principally from my having spit so much blood." He had not time, however, to waste many words with me, as he had plenty of others to attend. Dickenson, also, I found here; having been wounded, as I before told you. He did all he could to keep my spirits up, but, as you may suppose, I felt still very far from being comfortable. Nor were the various objects that met my eye of a consolatory nature: men lying, some dead, others at their last gasp, while the agonizing groans of those who were undergoing operations at the hands of the hospital assistants, added to the horror of the scene. I may now say that I have seen, on a small scale, every different feature of a fight.

In the meantime, there had been sharp fighting in the citadel. Our men, after forcing their way through numerous dark passages, in some places so narrow and low that they were forced to crawl singly on their hands and knees, at length arrived there; but as there were a great number of approaches to this their last place of refuge, our men got broken up into small detached parties, and entered it at different places. One party reached the place where Mehrab Khan, at the head of the chiefs who had joined his standard, was sitting with his sword drawn, &c. The others seemed inclined to surrender themselves, and raised the cry of "Amān!" but the Khan, springing on his feet, cried, "Amān, nag!" equivalent to "Mercy be d—d," and blew his match; but all in vain, as he immediately received about three shots, which completely did his business; the one that gave him the "*coup de grace*," and which went through his breast, being fired by a man of our regiment, named Maxwell. So fell Mehrab Khan, having fulfilled his promise to General Willshire, and died game, with his sword in his hand, in his own citadel.

Other parties, however, were not so fortunate, as each being too weak, the enemy generally offered a determined resistance, and several, after giving themselves up, finding the numbers to whom they had surrendered smaller than they had at first appeared, turned upon them suddenly; for which, however, they suffered in the long-run, as the soldiers, at last, maddened by this conduct, refused quarter, and fired at once into whatever party they met, without asking any questions.

At length the few survivors, being driven to their last stronghold at the very top of the citadel, surrendered on condition of their lives being granted to them; when one loud and general "hurrah!" proclaimed around that Kelat was ours. The greatest part of the garrison had, however, before this managed to make their escape over the hills. Dickenson, while he was lying wounded by my side, saw quantities of them letting themselves down the walls of the citadel by means of ropes, shawls, &c.

Dooly, the most faithful of his chiefs and followers, remained by Mehrab Khan to the last. These were all either taken prisoners or killed. Besides the Khan himself, the Dadur chief, who had been the cause of great annoyance to us in our way up, and the Governor of the Shawl district, were among the slain. The only two men of his council of any note among the survivors are at present prisoners in our camp, on their way to Bengal.

Thus ended this short, but decisive affair, which I consider to be a much more gallant one than that of Ghuzni, both in regard to the numbers engaged on each side and the manner in which it was taken. We merely halted for an hour, and then went slap at it, as if it was merely a continuation of our morning's march. General Willshire was exceedingly pleased with the result, as well he might be, and issued a very complimentary address to the force engaged, the next day. I hope and conclude his fortune will be made by it.

The loss on our side at Kelat was, in proportion, a great deal greater than at Ghuzni. We had altogether about 1100 bayonets engaged, and the loss was 140, being about one in seven; of this loss, the Queen's bear a proportion equal to that of the other two regiments together, having returned about seventy in the butcher's bill out of 280, which was the number we brought into the field, being about one in four. Out of thirteen officers, we had one killed, four severely, and one slightly, wounded; twenty-three men were killed, and forty-one wounded, of whom some have died since, and most will feel the effect of their wounds till their dying day, as the greatest portion are body wounds.

With regard to prize-money, I have no doubt that had things been even tolerably well managed, there would have been plenty of it, but we did not stay there long enough to search the place thoroughly. I hear also that the other part of the force that went down by the Bolan Pass claim to share with us, which we do not allow; so that, perhaps, it may get into the lawyers' hands, and then good-bye to it altogether. I do not expect, under any circumstances, more than 100*l.* Some of the rooms of the citadel were very handsomely fitted up, particularly one in the old fellow's harem, which was one entire mirror, both sides and ceiling.

We remained at Kelat till the 21st of November, and then marched by the Gundava Pass on this place. During the week that we remained there, my wounds continued doing very well, and I had very little fever; and on the third and fourth days after I was hit, the doctor considered me "all right." On the two first days of our march, however, I caught a low fever, which left me on the third, and I have continued to grow gradually better ever since. We found the Gundava a much longer and more difficult pass than that of the Bolan, and could get very little grain or supplies either for ourselves or our cattle. Our march was perfectly unmolested, as by that time the new Khan had arrived at Kelat, and most of the principal chiefs had acknowledged him. I do not know, however, what has become of Mehrab Khan's eldest son, a lad of fifteen years old, who was bringing up a reinforcement to his father in our rear, while we were marching on Kelat, but did not arrive in the neighbourhood until after the place was taken. He, however, threatened us with a night attack while we were lying in front of it, so that we were on the alert, every one sleeping on his arms during the whole time we were there.

"We laid not by our harness bright,
Neither by day nor yet by night."

During the whole of this time the weather set in dreadfully cold, colder than I ever experienced it anywhere in my life; sharp frosts, &c.

Well; to cut the matter short, yesterday, the 7th of December, we arrived at this place, which is the same that we halted at for a week in our march up. Here, at length, we are in the land of plenty, and enjoy such luxuries as fresh eggs, butter, milk, vegetables, &c., with a goût that those only can feel who have been so long without them as we have. We find the climate, however, very hot, and I am sorry to say that we are losing many fine fellows from the effect of the change. It is very painful to witness these poor fellows going off in this miserable manner, after surviving the chances of fire and steel, and all the harassing duties they have had to perform during the campaign, now when they have arrived at nearly the very end of it.

Larkhanu, Dec. 24th.—I have delayed sending this till our arrival here, as the communication between this and Bombay is perfectly open, which might not have been the case at Kotra. We have been here about a week, and report says that we are to finish our marching here, and drop down the river to Curachee in boats. I hope this may prove the case, as I am sure we have had marching enough for one campaign. Another report, however, says, that there is a kick-up in the Punjab, and that we shall be detained in this country in consequence; but I do not think it likely.

That part of our force which was not employed at Kelat went down by the Bolan Pass, and have suffered considerably from cholera, which luckily we have as yet escaped. The men that we have lost since our arrival in this low country have all died from complaints of the lungs, from which they were perfectly free in the cold country above the hills. Since writing the former part of this letter, I have received a letter from Kate, dated September 10th, which I will answer as soon I have finished this letter to you.

December 25th, Christmas day.—I hope to spend this evening more comfortably than I did last year, when I was on out-lying picket, the night before we commenced our first march. Now, I trust, we have finished our last. We have luckily met all our mess supplies here, which have been waiting for us about six months, having never managed to get further than Bukkur. So now it is a regular case of—

> "Who so merry as we in camp?
> Danger over,
> Live in clover," &c.

I have just heard that the order is out for our marching the day after to-morrow to the banks of the river, there to remain till the boats are ready. Now the campaign is so near its close, I feel very glad that

I have been on it, as it is a thing that a man does not see every day of his life in these times; and I consider it to be more lucky than otherwise that I have four holes in my body as a remembrance of it; but I cannot say that I relish a longer sojourn in India, unless we have the luck to be sent to China, which I should like very much, (fancy sacking Pekin, and kicking the Celestial Emperor from his throne,) as I do not think the climate has done me any good, but on the contrary.

I do not know whether these wounds of mine will give me any claim;—and, talking about that, I would wish you to inquire whether or not I am entitled to any gratuity for them. I hear that officers returned "wounded" on the list in the Peninsular Campaign, no matter how slight the wound might have been, received a gratuity of one year's pay as a compensation; and this, I think, was called "blood-money." I do not know how far this may be the case at present, but I do not think that 120*l.* ought to be lost sight of for want of a little inquiry.

By-the-bye, I had nearly forgotten to say that I have received two letters from Eliza, which I will answer as soon as possible; but I do not think it safe to keep this open any longer, as I may lose the mail to Bombay; so must conclude, with best love to all at home,

Your very affectionate son,

T. W. E. Holdsworth.

LETTER XI.

Camp, Larkanu, Dec. 26th, 1839.

My dear Eliza,—I finished and sent off a letter to my father yesterday, giving an account of the storming of Kelat, and the wounds I received in the skrimmage, and telling him of everything that had happened since I wrote before, which was the day we left Cabool. You can see his letter, which gives a pretty full account of all our proceedings up to the present time.

I have now to make many apologies for not having answered your two letters, one dated May 29th, giving an account of Kate's wedding, and the other, dated the 29th of July, from Bristol, and likewise for having forgotten to thank you for the money you were kind enough to send out with my father's, last year. I can assure you never came money more acceptable, as no one can imagine what expenses we have unavoidably been obliged to incur in this campaign, which I suppose has cost officers more than any other campaign that ever was undertaken. I think there are few of us who have come off under 100*l.* besides our pay; and yet this was merely for the common necessaries of life,—just sufficient to keep body and soul together. I can assure you I feel very much obliged for your present, as also for the two letters which I received while on the march. I have often thought of Brookhill during the many dreary marches that we have made, and on the solitary out-lying pickets, with no one to speak to, and deplored my unlucky fate, in being obliged to leave home just as you seem to be comfortably settled there. Still I have hope that I may yet return, some day or other.

I can now give you more definite intelligence with regard to our movements than I did in my father's letter, since sending off which orders have come out, and the campaign, as far as our regiment is concerned, is decidedly brought to a close. H. M. 17th, with Gen. Willshire, Baumgardt, and Head-quarter Staff, marched this morning for Bukkur, where they are to remain for four or five months, so report says, and longer than that I suppose, if their services are required. The Queen's, and the 4th Light Dragoons, are to return to Bombay as soon as the necessary arrangements for their transportation thither &c. are completed. We march from this to-morrow for the banks of the river, about twelve miles, and shall probably remain there for three weeks or so, until the shipping is got ready in Bombay, when we shall drop down the Indus in boats, and embark from Curachee for the Presidencies: would it were for England. Most of our married officers have obtained leave to precede the regiment, and are off in a day or two.

I hope to see Lieutenant-Colonel Fane when we arrive at Bombay. His father, Sir H. Fane, has publicly and officially resigned the commander-in-chief-ship in favour of Sir Jasper Nicolls. Sir Henry has been dangerously unwell at Bombay; but report says he is now getting better. He intends sailing as soon as possible, I believe, and so will most likely be gone before we arrive there. Sir J. Keane has also resigned, and is to be succeded by Sir Thomas M'Mahon. It is not quite certain that we shall go to Bombay, as some say that we shall land at Cambay, and go up to Deesa, and others that we shall return to Belgaum. Last night we received Bombay papers, giving an account of the taking of Kelat. They have buttered us up pretty well, and seem to think it a much more gallant affair than that of Ghuzni — in this last particular they are only doing us justice.

Dec. 30th, Camp, Taggur Bundur, Banks of the Indus.—We arrived here the day before yesterday, and are likely to remain, I believe, a fortnight or so. We muster rather small, as most of the married officers are off to-day and yesterday. As to my wounds, I have only one hole still open—namely, the one through which the bullet took its final departure, and that, I think, will be closed in a day or two. I am sorry to say that since arriving here I have caught a "cruel cold," from which I am suffering severely at present.

By-the-bye, there are a few incidents connected with the taking of Kelat which I forgot to mention in my letter to my father. Mehrab Khan, the chief of Kelat, managed to send away all his harem and family on the morning of the fight, directly we were seen approaching, but his other chiefs were not so fortunate, and the greater part of them deliberately cut the throats of all the females belonging to their establishments, including wives, mothers, and daughters, as soon as we established ourselves within the town, rather than suffer them to fall into the hands of us infidels. I forgot, I think, also, to mention that I managed to procure rather a handsome Koran, which was found in the citadel, and also an excellent Damascus blade, both of which I intend giving to my father, and a few articles of native costume, which would go far to make up a neat fancy dress, but it is not quite complete. A great number of handsome articles were stolen by the camp followers and other rascals, worse luck for us poor wounded officers, who could not help ourselves. We were rather surprised at finding some excellent European articles in the shape of double-barrelled guns, pistols, beautiful French musical boxes, prints, looking-glasses, and pier-glasses, &c., in the rooms of the citadel. Where Mehrab Khan could have picked them up I cannot think, unless they were the result of some successful foray on some unfortunate caravan.

The day after the fight, Captain Outram, of whom I have so often spoken in my letters to my father, volunteered to take the dispatches to Bombay, and started for that purpose straight across country to Someanee Bay, on the sea-coast, a distance of 350 miles, and across the barren mountains that compose the greatest part of Beloochistan. This route had up to that time never been traversed by any European, except Pottinger, who passed through all these countries twenty years ago, disguised as a native. It was attempted last year by Captain Harris, of the Bombay Engineers, author of the "African Excursions," a very enterprising officer, and who landed at Someanee Bay for that purpose; but after getting about twenty miles into the interior, reported the route as impracticable. When this is taken into consideration, with the great chance there was of Captain Outram's falling into the hands of the many straggling fugitives from Kelat, and the well-known character of these *gentlemen*, now smarting under the painful feeling of being driven from their homes, &c., it must be confessed that it required no little pluck to undertake it. The plan proved, however, perfectly successful. He travelled in the disguise of an Afghan Peer, or holy man, under the guidance of two Afghan Seyds, a race of men much looked up to and respected in all Mahomedan countries, on account of their obtaining, [whether true or not, I know not] a pure descent from the Prophet. Outram and his party fell in with several bands of fugitives, and actually came up and were obliged to travel a day or two with the harem and escort of Mehrab Khan's brother. As there was a chance of Outram's being discovered by this party, the Seyd introduced him in the character of a Peer, which holy disguise he had to support during the whole journey; and after some extraordinary escapes he arrived at Someanee Bay in seven or eight days.

Our sick and wounded have been left behind at Kelat, under the charge of an officer of the 17th, since which things have gone on very smoothly there. The new Khan has been very accommodating, and has given fêtes, &c., to the officers left behind, in honour of our gallantry. He has also written to General Willshire to say that he intends giving us all a medal each, whether we are allowed to wear it or not, as he does not see why, if the Shah did it for Ghuzni, he might not do it also for Kelat. Lord Auckland has published an order that all regiments belonging to the Company that went beyond the Bolan Pass shall wear Afghanistan on their colours and appointments, and all engaged at Ghuzni that name also; and has written to the Queen for permission for Queen's regiments employed in like manner to bear the same. I suppose we shall get Kelat in addition.

There is one other point which, in my hurry to get

my letter off in time for the January mail, I totally forgot to mention—viz., about drawing some money on my father. I have before mentioned the great expense we have been put to in this campaign; in addition to this, when we were ordered from Quettah to take Kelat, we were also under orders to return to Quettah after having taken the place. A sergeant was therefore left behind at Quettah to take charge of whatever effects any person might leave, and officers were strongly advised to leave the greater part of their kit at this place. I, as well as most of my brother officers, was foolish enough to follow this advice, and brought only a bundle of linen; consequently now I am almost minus everything; dress-coat, appointments, are all left behind, as General Willshire, after the taking of Kelat, instead of returning to Quettah, proceeded into Cutch Gundava by the Gundava Pass. Nothing has been since heard of what we have left behind, except that the sergeant could not get camels or carriage sufficient to bring them down. Moreover, it is unsafe to go through the Bolan Pass without a tolerably strong escort; so, taking all things into consideration, I do not think there is much chance of our ever seeing anything of them again. The consequences will be, that, on our arrival at Bombay, I shall be obliged to get an entire new fit out, and as the campaign has drained me dry, I shall be obliged to draw upon my father for it; however, I will repay him by the end of the year, as by that time the Company will have given us half a year's full batta, which they intend doing as a sort of indemnification for the losses we have sustained on the campaign; my batta will be about 72*l.*

I do not think I have any more to say, and as the January overland sails on the 25th, I hope this letter will reach Bombay in time to go by it, as well as my father's. By-the-bye, how is old Nelly? If she has any good pups, I wish you would manage to keep one for me, as I expect the old girl will be either dead or very old by the time I return. I am longing to get out of the "Sick-list," as the thickets here near the river are full of partridges and hares, and the climate, at this time of the year, is very cool and pleasant. My rheumatism is much better since I was wounded; but I still have it in my left arm. Well, no more; but wishing you, and all, a happy new year.

Believe me ever your very affectionate brother,

T. W. E. HOLDSWORTH.

LETTER XII.

Camp, Curachee, Feb. 14th, 1840.

My dear Father,—You will see, by my date, that our share of the campaign is ended; in fact, we are only waiting here for shipping, which is on its way from Bombay, to take us from this place to Mandavie, in Cutch, where we land, and then march immediately to Deesa, in Guzerat; so that, after all our toilsome marches, &c., we have yet another, still more toilsome, before us of 240 miles. The climate of Cutch and Guzerat during the period of year that we shall be occupied in marching is so hot that no changes of station are ever made even by native corps, and Europeans are never allowed to march in Guzerat except during the cold months. It is sharp work on our poor men; many of whom appear very unfit for it; but they are now so accustomed to hard work, that they will get well through it I have little doubt.

We left Tuggur Bandur, from which place I wrote to Eliza and Kate, on the 13th of January, and drifted quietly down the river in boats, pulling up and coming to an anchor every evening at sunset. We reached Tatta Bundur, about five miles from the town, on the 21st, and after staying there a few days, started again for this place, which we reached in five marches, on the 31st. We were immediately most hospitably entertained by the officers of H. M. 40th, which is an excellent regiment. Here we have been ever since, living on the fat of the land, and enjoying ourselves very much, after all our toils. This is now a rather considerable station: one Queen's and one Company's regiment, and detail of foot artillery, and plenty of European supplies brought by the Bombay merchants. It is a very decent climate, and would make a very good station. I wish they would leave us here in place of sending us to Deesa, at this time of the year. Sir John Keane, General Willshire, and the Bombay staff are expected here in a day or two. Sir John is bringing down with him Hyder Khan, Dost Mahomed's son, who commanded at Ghuzni when it was taken. He is to be brought to Bombay, and as he is of a very quiet, amiable disposition, will, so report says, be eventually allowed to join his father. Poor Dost, they say, is in a very bad way, deserted by nearly all his followers; but there still seems to be mischief brewing in the north-west. All accounts say that Bokhara is very much inclined to the Russian interest, and Shah Kamran's vizier at Herat has been carrying on a correspondence with the Persians, the object of which is said to be the delivery of Herat into their hands. The Punjab is also in a very unsettled state; so there are plenty of materials for getting up another row in these countries before long. War is most positively said to be decided on with China, and seven regiments, to be followed by a reserve of equal number, together with a considerable naval force, are to be sent there as soon as possible. Lord Auckland, we are told, has had *carte blanche* from the Home government to act as he thinks fit with regard to China, and that he has determined upon a hostile movement as soon as this campaign is regularly finished, which it may be said to be; so there will be glorious fun there. It is not yet known here what regiments will go. I am afraid there is little chance for the Queen's.

The 4th Light Dragoons have arrived here, having come down by land; they are to return to their old quarters at Kickee, near Poonah. The 17th may also be expected in a few days; they are to occupy our old quarters at Belgaum. The 18th (Royal Irish) have come on from Ceylon, and are to go to Poonah; and the 6th go home (to England) as soon as possible. This is understood to be the destination of each regiment, but this affair with China may cause an alteration.

I am very sorry to mention the unfortunate death of poor little Halkett, one of my best friends, and the son of General Halkett, of Hanover, who was so very civil to me while I was there, and nephew of Sir Colin Halkett.

Since we have been here, I have received your letter, dated November 2nd, by which it appears that you had just then heard of the taking of Ghuzni. You mentioned, also, in it that you had received my letter from Candahar, which I am very glad to hear, as I was very much afraid, from the state of the country, that it would never reach its destination. As you mention nothing about it, I suppose you had not received the letter I wrote from Ghuzni almost immediately after the capture. I know many letters were lost about that time, and mine, I am afraid, among the number. There is a report here (but I think, too good to be true) that all officers with the advance, or storming, party at Ghuzni, consisting of the light companies of the European regiments, were to get brevet rank. In that case, as the company to which I belong—viz., the Light—was one of the number, and, in fact, headed the assault, Capt. Holdsworth would be my future rank. Tell Eliza that I got her letter, which was enclosed in yours, and was very much surprised at its contents.

I do not know what to say about Deesa as a station, reports are so various on the subject. The heat, I believe, is awful in the hot weather, the thermometer rising to 120 in the houses; and the worst part of the business is, that this heat, which is occasioned by the hot winds, lasts all night through; so that the night is nearly as hot as the day. At other times of the year, I believe, the climate is very pleasant. The 40th give a very good account of it. There is a great quantity of game there, and some of the best hog-hunting in India. Mount Aboo, called the Parnassus of India, is within fifty miles of it, and is a great place of resort during the hot weather.

Should this expedition to China take place, which seems decided upon at present, what an immense power the English will eventually have in the East. In a few years, I have no doubt it may extend from Herat to the most eastern parts of China, including all the islands in the adjacent seas. Like the Romans, England seems to be extending her dominion everywhere—"super et Garamantes et Indos, proferet imperium," and yet what a row she kicks up about Russia. The French papers seem to be rather jealous about Ghuzni. How the English papers butter it up! and yet it was not half so brilliant an affair as Kelat, nor so hardly contested; but very little is said about the latter.

Enclosed, I send you a view of the north front of Kelat, shewing the gate by which we entered. It gives you a pretty good idea of the place, and was drawn by Lieutenant Creed, of the Engineers.

I went yesterday to see a tank, about seven miles

from this place, in which are a great quantity of alligators, half tame. The tank in which they are belongs to a Mahomedan temple, which is considered a very holy one, and much resorted to, and these animals are kept there by the priests of the establishment, in order to induce a greater number of visitors. A calf was killed and thrown in among the scaly gentlemen, who very soon demolished it. I never saw anything so loathesome and repulsive as these monsters.

This letter goes by the "Hannah" packet, which sails this evening for Bombay, and will, I hope, reach that place in time to go by the "overland packet." I suppose you know that this is classic ground, and the place from which Nearchus, Alexander's admiral, started on his return to the Euphrates. I have no time for more. So, with love to all at home,

Believe me your affectionate son,

T. W. E. Holdsworth.

LETTER XIII.

Deesa, April 21st, 1840.

My dear Father,—I received your letter, dated January 18th, about the beginning of this month, while on our march from Mandavie to this place. I see by the papers that the news of the taking of Kelat had reached England, as I find my name mentioned in the "Western Luminary," which came out in this overland. I wrote you last from Curachee, about the beginning or middle of February. We stayed there till the 20th. A few days before we left, Lord Keane and suite arrived, bringing with him Hyder Khan, the captured chief of Ghuzni. While there, Lord Keane presented new colours to the 40th regiment, which we had an opportunity of witnessing. He and all his party have since gone home.

On the 20th, I, with my company under my command, embarked for Mandavie, in Cutch, where we arrived in two days, in Patamars, and waited till the whole regiment came down, which they did by companies, so that it was the 10th of March before we were able to start for this place.

We arrived here on the 4th of this month, pushing on as fast as we could, as the commanding officer was anxious to get the men under cover, on account of the great heat. There was excellent shooting the whole way up; and if it had been the cold season, I should have enjoyed the march amazingly; but it was too hot to venture out. On arrival here we found about three hundred recruits, who had arrived since we went on service, and about fifty of the men we left behind us; also seven new officers. As I have a company under my command I have scarcely had a moment to myself since I have been here; what with fitting and getting the recruits in order, and new clothing the old hands, you have no conception what tedious work it is getting into quarters.

I have bought a very comfortable little bungalo for four hundred rupees. We were promised our full batta on our arrival here; but, although the Bengalees, it is said, received theirs some time ago, yet there is a screw loose, I fear, somewhere in the Bombay, and that it may be some time before we get ours, and that it will not be as much as the Bengalees: so much for being in an inferior Presidency. This is a great disappointment, after our losses on the campaign.

With regard to this place, I have not been long

enough in it to form an opinion. Its appearance is decidedly against it, the soil being nothing but a barren sandy desert, with the low hills of the Aravulles to the eastward, running north to the mountain Aboo, the Parnassus of Hindostan. The last week has been oppressive, and hot in the extreme; and this is but the commencement of the hot weather, which I am told will last about six weeks longer, when a very slight monsoon comes on, and lasts at intervals till the end of October, when the cold season commences, which is said to be very pleasant. There is a lot of game here of every description, including lions; and it is one of the best hog-hunting stations in India.

Our men, to the surprise of everybody, were very healthy in the march up; and since they have been here, and not having their knapsacks to carry, knocked off their work in grand style. The men we have brought back with us are well-seasoned, hardy fellows, and I would back them to march against any soldiers in the world.

I suppose you have long ere this received Stisted's letter and mine about Kelat. Colonel Arnold* died at Cabool whilst we were there, and was buried with a magnificent military funeral in the Armenian burial-

* Colonel Arnold was in the 10th Hussars at Waterloo, and shot through the body in the charge in which Major Howard, of that regiment, was killed.

ground. I am sorry to say that, as I predicted, the spear which I took at the storming of Ghuzni has been broken to pieces through the carelessness of my servants. I have, however, the Koran and sword from Kelat; and I think I shall be able to get a matchlock taken at that place,—a very good specimen of the sort of thing I was wounded by; perhaps it may be the identical one. The sword I left in Cutch, in my way up from Mandavie, to be put to rights, as the workmen of that country are the best in India. I will try if I can get another weapon, as a remembrance of Ghuzni. I brought down from Cabool as far as Quettah a very good specimen of the Kyber knife, a very cut-throat sort of instrument, with which every Afghan is armed. I sent it down with my other things through the Bolan Pass, when we turned off to Kelat, and I am sorry to say it was stolen.

You write about old * * * * *: did I never mention him to you? He is here; but was not with us on the campaign, being too unwell when we started. Though not an old man, he is a very old soldier for an Indian, and is nearly worn out: he is anxious to get his discharge at the end of the year, when he will have served his twenty-one years, and be entitled to a decent pension. He is a very straight-forward, blunt, honest old fellow, and when he first joined was a very powerful man, and the best wrestler in the regiment, thereby proving his South Devon blood. He was * * * * *'s servant when I joined, and I was delighted at hearing the South Devon dialect again, which he speaks with so much truth and native elegance that you would imagine he had but just left his native village. There were a great many Devonshire men in the regiment; we lost one, a very fine young man in the Grenadiers, in coming down from Kelat to Cutch Gundava, by the same chest complaint that carried off so many: he was a native of Tiverton.

Well; it is twelve o'clock, and I am afraid I shall be too late for the post; so good bye.

Your affectionate son,

T. W. E. Holdsworth.

APPENDIX.

APPENDIX.

FALL OF GHUZNI, & ENTRANCE OF THE BRITISH ARMY INTO CABOOL.

(*From the Bombay Government Gazette Extraordinary of August 29th,* 1839.)

SECRET DEPARTMENT.

Bombay Castle, Aug. 29th, 1839.

The Honourable the Governor in Council has the highest satisfaction in republishing the following notification issued by the Right Honourable the Governor-General, announcing the capture by storm of the town and fortress of Ghuzni, as also the general order issued on the occasion by his Excellency Lieutenant-General Sir John Keane, K.C.B. and G.C.H., Commander-in-Chief of the Army of the Indus. By order of the Honourable the Governor in Council,

L. R. Reid, Acting Chief Secretary.

NOTIFICATION.—SECRET DEPARTMENT.

Simla, August 18th, 1839.

The Right Hon. the Governor-General of India has great gratification in publishing, for general information, a copy of a report this day received from his Excellency Lieutenant-General Sir John Keane, K.C.B., Commander-in-Chief of the Army of the Indus, announcing the capture, by storm, on the 23d ult., of the important fortress of Ghuzni.

A salute of twenty-one guns will be fired on the receipt of this intelligence at all the principal stations of the army in the three Presidencies. By order of the Right Hon. the Governor-General of India,

(Signed) T. H. Maddock,
Officiating Secretary to the Government of India, with the Governor-General.

TO THE RIGHT HON. LORD AUCKLAND, G.C.B., ETC.

My Lord,—I have the satisfaction to acquaint your Lordship that the army under my command have succeeded in performing one of the most brilliant acts it has ever been my lot to witness during my service of forty-five years in the four quarters of the globe, in the capture, by storm, of the strong and important fortress and citadel of Ghuzni yesterday.

It is not only that the Afghan nation, and, I understand, Asia generally have looked upon it as impregnable ; but it is in reality a place of great strength, both by nature and art, far more so than I had reason to suppose from any description that I had received of it, although some are from officers in our own service who had seen it in their travels.

I was surprised to find a high rampart in good repair, built on a scarped mound about thirty-five feet high, flanked by numerous towers, and surrounded by a fausse brayze and a wet ditch, whilst the height of the citadel covered the interior from the commanding fire of the hills from the north, rendering it nugatory. In addition to this, screen walls had been built before the gates, the ditch was filled with water, and unfordable, and an outwork built on the right bank of the river so as to command the bed of it.

It is therefore the more honourable to the troops, and must appear to the enemy out of all calculation extraordinary, that a fortress and citadel to the strength of which, for the last thirty years, they had been adding something each year, and which had a garrison of 3500 Afghan soldiers, commanded by Prince Mahomed Hyder, the son of Dost Mahomed Khan, the ruler of the country, with a commanding number of guns, and abundance of ammunition, and other stores, provisions, &c., for a regular siege, should have been taken by British science and British valour in less than two hours from the time the attack was made, and the whole, including the governor and garrison, should fall into our hands.

My dispatch of the 20th instant, from Nanee, will have made known to your Lordship that the camps of his Majesty Shah Shooja-ool-Moolk, and of Major-General Willshire, with the Bombay troops, had there joined me in accordance with my desire, and the following morning we made our march of twelve miles to Ghuzni, the line of march being over a fine plain. The troops were disposed in a manner that would have enabled me at any moment, had we been attacked, as was probable, from the large bodies of troops moving on each side of us, to have placed them in position to receive the enemy. They did not, however, appear; but on our coming within range of the guns of the citadel and fortress of Ghuzni, a sharp cannonade was opened on our leading column, together with a heavy fire of musketry from behind garden walls, and temporary field-works thrown up, as well as the strong outwork I have already alluded to, which commanded the bed of the river from all but the outwork. The enemy were driven in under the walls of the fort in a spirited manner by parties thrown forward by Major-General Sir Willoughby Cotton, of the 16th and 48th Bengal Native Infantry, and her Majesty's 13th Light Infantry, under Brigadier Sale. I ordered forward three troops of horse artillery, the camel battery, and one foot battery, to open upon the citadel and fortress, by throwing shrapnel shells, which was done in a masterly style under the direction of Brigadier Stephenson. My object in this was to make the enemy shew their strength in guns, and in other respects, which completely succeeded, and our shells must have done great execution, and occasioned great consternation. Being perfectly satisfied on the point of their strength in the course of half an hour, I ordered the fire to cease, and placed the troops in bivouac. A close reconnoissance of the place all around was then undertaken by Captain Thomson, the chief engineer, and Captain Peat, of the Bombay Engineers, accompanied by Major Garden, the Deputy Quarter-master-General of the Bombay army, supported by a strong party of her Majesty's 16th Lancers, and one from her Majesty's 18th Light Infantry. On this party a steady fire was kept up, and some casualties occurred. Captain Thomson's report was very clear; he found the fortifications equally strong all round; and, as my own opinion coincided with his, I did not hesitate a moment as to the manner in which our approach and attack upon the place should be made. Notwithstanding the march the troops had performed in the morning, and their having been a considerable time engaged with the enemy, I ordered the whole to move across the river (which runs close under the fort wall) in columns, to the right and left of the town, and they were placed in opposition on the north side on more commanding ground, and securing the Cabool road. I had information that a night attack upon the camp was intended from without. Mahomed Ubzul Khan, the eldest son of Dost Mahomed Khan, had been sent by his father with a strong body of troops from Cabool to the brother's assistance at Ghuzni, and was encamped outside the walls, but abandoned his position on our approach, keeping, however, at the distance of a few miles from us. The two rebel chiefs of the Ghiljee tribe, men of great influence—viz., Abdool Rhuman and Gool Mahomed Khan, had joined him with 1500 horse, and also a body of about 3000 Ghazees from Zeimat, under a mixture of chiefs and mollahs, carrying banners, and who had been assembled on the cry of a religious war. In short, we were in all directions surrounded by enemies. These last actually came down the hills on the 22nd, and attacked the part of the camp occupied by his Majesty Shah Shooja and his own troops, but were driven back with considerable loss, and banners taken.

At daylight on the 22nd I reconnoitered Ghuzni, in company with the chief engineer and the brigadier commanding the artillery, with the adjutant and quartermaster-general of the Bengal army, for the purpose of making all arrangements for carrying the place by storm, and these were completed in the course of the day. Instead of the tedious process of breaching, (for which we were ill prepared,) Captain Thomson undertook, with the assistance of Captain Peat, of the Bombay Engineers, Lieutenants Durand and Macleod, of the Bengal Engineers, and other officers under him, (Captain Thomson,) to blow in the Cabool gate, the weakest point, with gunpowder; and so much faith did I place on the success of this operation that my plans for the assault were immediately laid down and the orders given.

The different troops of horse artillery, the camel and foot batteries, moved off their ground at twelve o'clock that night, without the slightest noise, as had been directed, and in the most correct manner took up the position assigned them, about 250 yards from the walls. In like manner, and with the same silence, the infantry soon after moved from their ground, and all were at their post at the proper time. A few minutes before three o'clock in the morning the explosion took place, and proved completely successful. Captain Peat, of the Bombay Engineers, was thrown down and stunned by it, but shortly after recovered his senses and feeling. On hearing the advance sounded by the bugle, (being the signal for the gate having been blown in,) the artillery, under the able directions of Brigadier Stevenson, consisting of Captain Grant's troop of Bengal Horse Artillery, the camel battery, under Captain Abbott, both superintended by Major Pew, Captains Martin and Cotgrave's troops of Bombay Horse Artillery, and Captain Lloyd's battery of Bombay Foot Artillery, all opened a terrific fire upon the citadel and ramparts of the fort, and, in a certain degree, paralysed the enemy.

Under the guidance of Captain Thomson, of the Bengal Engineers, the chief of the department, Colonel Dennie, of her Majesty's 13th Light Infantry, commanding the advance, consisting of the light companies of her Majesty's 2nd and 17th regiments of Foot, and of the Bengal European regiment, with one company of her Majesty's 13th Light Infantry, proceeded to the gate, and with great difficulty, from the rubbish thrown down, and the determined opposition offered by the enemy, effected an entrance, and established themselves within the gateway, closely followed by the main column, led in a spirit of great gallantry by Brigadier Sale, to whom I had entrusted the important post of commanding the storming party, consisting (with the advance above-mentioned) of her Majesty's 2nd Foot, under Major Carruthers; the Bengal European regiment, under Lieutenant-Colonel Orchard, followed by her Majesty's 13th Light Infantry, under Major Tronson; and her Majesty's 17th regiment, under Lieutenant-Colonel Croker. The struggle within the fort was desperate for a considerable time. In addition to the heavy fire kept up, our troops were assailed by the enemy sword in hand, and with daggers, pistols, &c.; but British courage, perseverance, and fortitude, overcame all opposition, and the fire of the enemy in the lower area of the fort being nearly silenced, Brigadier Sale turned towards the citadel, from which could now be seen men abandoning the guns, running in all directions, throwing themselves down from immense heights, endeavouring to make their escape; and on reaching the gate with her Majesty's 17th, under Lieutenant-Colonel Croker, followed by the 13th, forced it open at five o'clock in the morning. The colours of her Majesty's 13th and 17th were planted on the citadel of Ghuzni amidst the cheers of all ranks. Instant protection was granted to the women found in the citadel, (among whom were those of Mahomed Hyder, the governor,) and sentries placed over the magazine for its security. Brigadier Sale reports having received much assistance from Captain Kershaw, of her Majesty's 13th Light Infantry, throughout the whole of the service of the storming.

Major-General Sir Willoughby Cotton executed in a manner much to my satisfaction the orders he had received. The Major-General followed closely the assaulting party into the fort with the reserve—namely, Brigadier Roberts, with the only available regiment of his brigade; the 35th Native Infantry, under Lieutenant-Colonel Monteath; part of Brigadier Sale's brigade, the 16th Native Infantry, under Major Maclaren; and 48th Native Infantry, under Lieutenant-Colonel Wheeler; and they immediately occupied the ramparts, putting down opposition whenever they met any, and making prisoners, until the place was completely in our possession. A desultory fire was kept up in the town long after the citadel was in our hands, from those who had taken shelter in houses, and in desperation kept firing on all that approached them. In this way several of our men were wounded, and some killed, but the aggressors paid dearly for their bad conduct in not surrendering when the place was completely ours. I must not omit to mention that three companies of the 35th Native Infantry, under Captain Hay, ordered to the south side of the fort to begin with a false attack, to attract attention on that side, performed that service at the proper time, and greatly to my satisfaction.

As we were threatened with an attack for the relief of the garrison, I ordered the 19th Bombay Native Infantry, under the command of Lieutenant-Colonel Stalker, to guard the Cabool road, and to be in support of the cavalry division. This might have proved an important position to occupy, but as it was, no enemy appeared.

The cavalry division, under Major-General Thackwell, in addition to watching the approach of an enemy, had directions to surround Ghuzni, and to sweep the plain, preventing the escape of runaways from the garrison. Brigadier Arnold's brigade—the Brigadier himself, I deeply regret to say, was labouring under very severe illness, having shortly before burst a blood-vessel internally, which rendered it wholly impossible for him to mount a horse that day—consisting of her Majesty's 16th Lancers, under Lieutenant-Colonel Persse, temporarily commanding the brigade, and Major

Mac Dowell, the junior major of the regiment, (the senior major of the 16th Lancers, Major Cureton, an officer of great merit, being actively engaged in the execution of his duties as Assistant Adjutant-General to the cavalry division,) the 2nd Cavalry, under Major Salter, and the 3rd, under Lieutenant-Colonel Smith, were ordered to watch the south and west sides. Brigadier Scott's brigade were placed on the Cabool road, consisting of her Majesty's 4th Light Dragoons, under Major Daly, and of the 1st Bombay Cavalry, under Lieutenant-Colonel Sandwith, to watch the north and east sides: this duty was performed in a manner greatly to my satisfaction.

After the storming, and that quiet was in some degree restored within, I conducted his Majesty Shah Shooja-ool-Moolk, and the British Envoy and Minister, Mr. Macnaghten, round the citadel and a great part of the fortress. The king was perfectly astonished at our having made ourselves masters of a place conceived to be impregnable, when defended, in the short space of two hours, and in less than forty-eight hours after we came before it. His Majesty was, of course, greatly delighted at the result. When I afterwards, in the course of the day, took Mahomed Hyder Khan, the governor, first to the British Minister, and then to the King, to make his submission, I informed his Majesty that I had made a promise that his life should not be touched, and the King, in very handsome terms, assented, and informed Mahomed Hyder, in my presence, that although he and his family had been rebels, yet he was willing to forget and forgive all.

Prince Mahomed Hyder, the Governor of Ghuzni, is a prisoner of war in my camp, and under the surveillance of Sir Alexander Burnes, an arrangement very agreeable to the former.

From Major-General Sir W. Cotton, commanding the 1st infantry division, (of the Bengal army,) I have invariably received the strongest support; and on this occasion his exertions were manifest in support of the honour of the profession and of our country.

I have likewise, at all times, received able assistance from Major-

General Willshire, commanding the 2nd infantry division, (of the Bombay army,) which it was found expedient on that day to break up, some for the storming party, and some for other duties. The Major-General, as directed, was in attendance upon myself.

To Brigadier Sale I feel deeply indebted for the gallant and soldierlike manner in which he conducted the responsible and arduous duty entrusted to him in command of the storming party, and for the arrangements he made in the citadel immediately after taking possession of it. The sabre wound which he received in the face did not prevent his continuing to direct his column until everything was secure; and I am happy in the opportunity of bringing to your Lordship's notice the excellent conduct of Brigadier Sale on this occasion.

Brigadier Stevenson, in command of the Artillery, was all I could wish; and he reports that Brigade-Majors Backhouse and Coghlan ably assisted him. His arrangements were good; and the execution done by the arm he commands, was such as cannot be forgotten by those of the enemy who have witnessed and survived it.

To Brigadier Roberts, to Colonel Dennie, who commanded the advance, and to the different officers commanding regiments already mentioned, as well as to the other officers, and gallant soldiers under them, who so nobly maintained the honour and reputation of our country, my best acknowledgments are due.

To Captain Thomson, of the Bengal Engineers, the chief of the department with me, much of the credit of the success of this brilliant *coup-de-main* is due. A place of the same strength, and by such simple means as this highly-talented and scientific officer recommended to be tried, has, perhaps, never before been taken; and I feel I cannot do sufficient justice to Captain Thomson's merits for his conduct throughout. In the execution he was ably supported by the officers already mentioned; and so eager were the other officers of the Engineers of both Presidencies for the honour of carrying the powder bags, that the point could only be decided by seniority, which shews the fine feeling by which they were animated.

I must now inform your Lordship, that since I joined the Bengal column in the Valley of Shawl, I have continued my march with it in the advance; and it has been my good fortune to have had the assistance of two most efficient staff-officers in Major Craigie, Deputy Adjutant-General, and Major Garden, Deputy Quartermaster-General. It is but justice to those officers that I should state to your Lordship the high satisfaction I have derived from the manner in which all their duties have been performed up to this day, and that I look upon them as promising officers to fill the higher ranks. To the other officers of both departments I am also much indebted for the correct performance of all duties appertaining to their situations.

To Major Keith, the Deputy Adjutant-General, and Major Campbell, the Deputy Quartermaster-General of the Bombay army, and to all the other officers of both departments under them, my acknowledgments are also due, for the manner in which their duties have been performed during this campaign.

Captain Alexander, commanding the 4th Bengal Local Horse, and Major Cunningham, commanding the Poona Auxiliary Horse, with the men under their orders, have been of essential service to the army in this campaign.

The arrangements made by Superintending-Surgeons Kennedy and Atkinson previous to the storming, for affording assistance and comfort to the wounded, met with my approval.

Major Parsons, the Deputy Commissary-General, in charge of the department in the field, has been unremitting in his attention to keep the troops supplied, although much difficulty is experienced, and he is occasionally thwarted by the nature of the country and its inhabitants.

I have throughout this service received the utmost assistance I could derive from Lieutenant-Colonel Macdonald, my officiating military secretary, and Deputy Adjutant-General of her Majesty's Forces, Bombay; from Captain Powell, my Persian interpreter, and the other officers of my personal staff. The nature of the country in which we are serving, prevents the possibility of my sending a single staff-officer to deliver this to your Lordship, otherwise I should have asked my aide-de-camp, Lieutenant Keane, to proceed to Simla, to deliver this despatch into your hands, and to have afforded any further information that your Lordship could have desired.

The brilliant triumph we have obtained, the cool courage displayed, and the gallant bearing of the troops I have the honour to command, will have taught such a lesson to our enemies in the Afghan nation as will make them hereafter respect the name of a British soldier.

Our loss is wonderfully small considering the occasion; the casualties in killed and wounded amount to about 200.

The loss of the enemy is immense; we have already buried of their dead nearly 500, together with an immense number of horses.

I enclose a list of the killed, wounded, and missing. I am happy to say that, although the wounds of some of the officers are severe, they are all doing well.

It is my intention, after selecting a garrison for this place, and establishing a general hospital, to continue my march to Cabool forthwith.—I have, &c.,

(Signed) John Keane, Lieut.-General.

No. 1.

List of killed, wounded, and missing, in the army under the command of Lieutenant-General Sir John Keane, before Ghuzni, on the 21st of July, 1839 :—

2nd Troop Bengal Horse Artillery—3 horses wounded.

3rd Troop Bombay—2 rank and file, 2 horses, wounded.

4th Troop Bombay—1 horse killed.

2nd Regiment Bengal Cavalry—1 horse killed, 1 rank and file wounded.

4th Bengal Local Horse—1 rank and file and 1 horse missing.

Her Majesty's 13th Light Infantry—1 rank and file killed.

16th Bengal Native Infantry—1 captain wounded.

48th Ditto ditto—1 lieutenant, and 2 rank and file wounded

Total killed—1 rank and file, and two horses.

Total wounded—1 captain, 1 lieutenant, 5 rank and file, and 6 horses.

Total missing—1 rank and file, and 1 horse.

Names of Officers wounded.

Captain Graves, 16th Bengal Native Infantry, severely.

Lieutenant Vanhomrigh, 48th Bengal Native Infantry, slightly.

(Signed) R. Macdonald, Lieut.-Colonel,
Military Secretary, and Deputy Adjutant-Gen. to her Majesty's Forces, Bombay.

No. 2.

List of killed, wounded, and missing, in the army under the command of Lieutenant-General Sir John Keane, K.C.B. and G.C.H., in the assault and capture of the fortress and citadel of Ghuzni, on the 23rd of July, 1839:—

General Staff—1 colonel, 1 major, wounded.

3rd Troop Bombay Horse Artillery—1 rank and file wounded.

4th Ditto ditto—1 rank and file and 1 horse wounded.

Bengal Engineers—3 rank and file killed, 2 rank and file wounded, 1 rank and file missing.

Bombay Engineers—1 lieutenant, 1 rank and file, wounded.

2nd Bengal Light Cavalry—1 rank and file wounded.

1st Bombay Light Cavalry—1 havildar killed, 5 rank and file and 7 horses wounded.

Her Majesty's 2nd Foot (or Queen's Royals)—4 rank and file killed; 2 captains, 4 lieutenants, 1 sergeant, and 26 rank and file wounded.

Her Majesty's 13th Light Infantry—1 rank and file killed; 3 sergeants and 27 rank and file wounded.

Her Majesty's 17th Foot—6 rank and file wounded.

Bengal European Regiment—1 rank and file killed ; 1 lieutenant-colonel, 1 major, 2 captains, 4 lieutenants, 1 ensign, 1 sergeant, 51 rank and file wounded.

16th Bengal N. I.—1 havildar, 6 rank and file, wounded.

35th Ditto—5 rank and file killed ; 1 havildar and 8 rank and file wounded.

48th Ditto—2 havildars killed, 5 rank and file wounded.

Total killed—3 sergeants or havildars, 14 rank and file.

Total wounded—1 colonel, 1 lieutenant-colonel, 2 majors, 4 captains, 8 lieutenants, 2 ensigns, 7 sergeants or havildars, 140 rank and file, 8 horses.

Total missing—1 rank and file.

Grand total on the 21st and 23rd of July, killed, wounded, and missing—191 officers and men, and 16 horses.

Names of Officers killed, wounded, and missing.

General Staff—Brigadier Sale, her Majesty's 13th Light Infantry, slightly ; Major Parsons, Deputy Commissary-General, slightly.

Bombay Engineers—Second Lieutenant Marriott, slightly.

Her Majesty's 2nd (or Queen's Royals)—Captain Raitt, slightly ; Captain Robinson, severely ; Lieutenant Yonge, severely ; Lieut. Stisted, slightly ; Adjutant Simmons, slightly ; Quartermaster Hadley, slightly.

Bengal European Regiment — Lieutenant-Colonel Orchard, slightly ; Major Warren, severely ; Captains Hay and Taylor, slightly ; Lieutenant Broadfoot, slightly ; Lieutenant Haslewood, severely ; Lieutenants Fagan and Magnay, slightly ; Ensign Jacob, slightly.

(Signed) R. Macdonald, Lieut.-Colonel,

Military Secretary, and Deputy Adjutant-Gen. to her Majesty's Forces, Bombay.

GENERAL ORDER,

By his Excellency Lieutenant-Gen. Sir John Keane, Commander-in-Chief of the Army of the Indus.

Head-Quarters, Camp, Ghuzni, July 23rd, 1839.

Lieutenant-General Sir John Keane most heartily congratulates the army he has the honour to command, on the signal triumph they have this day obtained in the capture by storm of the strong and important fortress of Ghuzni. His Excellency feels that he can hardly do justice to the gallantry of the troops.

The scientific and successful manner in which the Cabool gate (of great strength) was blown up by Captain Thomson, of the Bengal Engineers, the chief of that department with this army, in which he reports having been most ably assisted by Captain Peat, of the Bombay Engineers, and Lieutenants Durand and Mac Leod, of the Bengal Engineers, in the daring and dangerous enterprise of laying down powder in the face of the enemy, and the strong fire kept up on them, reflects the highest credit on their skill and cool courage, and his Excellency begs Captain Thomson and officers named will accept his cordial thanks. His acknowledgments are also due to the other officers of the Engineers of both Presidencies, and to the valuable corps of Sappers and Miners under them. This opening having been made, although it was a difficult one to enter by, from the rubbish in the way, the leading column, in a spirit of true gallantry, directed and led by Brigadier Sale, gained a footing inside the fortress, although opposed by the Afghan soldiers in very great strength, and in the most desperate manner, with every kind of weapon.

The advance, under Lieutenant-Colonel Dennie, of her Majesty's 13th, consisting of the light companies of her Majesty's 2nd and 17th, and of the Bengal European Regiment, with one company of her Majesty's 13th; and the leading column, consisting of her Majesty's 2nd Queen's, under Major Carruthers, and the Bengal

European Regiment, under Lieutenant-Colonel Orchard, followed by her Majesty's 13th Light Infantry, as they collected from the duty of skirmishing, which they were directed to begin with, and by her Majesty's 17th, under Lieutenant-Colonel Croker. To all these officers, and to the other officers and gallant soldiers under their orders, his Excellency's best thanks are tendered; but, in particular, he feels deeptly indebted to Brigadier Sale, for the manner in which he conducted the arduous duty entrusted to him in the command of the storming party. His Excellency will not fail to bring it to the notice of his Lordship the Governor-General; and he trusts the wound which Brigadier Sale has received is not of that severe nature long to deprive this army of his services. Brigadier Sale reports that Captain Kershaw, of her Majesty's 13th Light Infantry, rendered important assistance to him and to the service in the storming.

Sir John Keane was happy, on this proud occasion, to have the assistance of his old comrade, Major-General Sir Willoughby Cotton, who, in command of the reserve, ably executed the instructions he had received, and was at the gate ready to enter after the storming party had established themselves inside, when he moved through it to sweep the ramparts, and to complete the subjugation of the place with the 16th Bengal Native Infantry, under Major M'Laren; Brigadier Roberts, with the 35th Native Infantry, under Lieutenant-Colonel Monteath; and the 48th Native Infantry, under Lieutenant-Colonel Wheeler. His arrangements afterwards, in continuation of those Brigadier Sale had made for the security of the magazine and other public stores, were such as meet his Excellency's high approval.

The Commander-in-Chief acknowledges the services rendered by Captain Hay, of the 35th Native Infantry, in command of three companies of that regiment sent to the south side of the fortress to begin with a false attack, and which was executed at the proper time, and in a manner highly satisfactory to his Excellency.

Nothing could be more judicious than the manner in which Brigadier Stevenson placed the artillery in position. Captain Grant's troop of Bengal Artillery, and the camel battery, under Captain Abbott, both superintended by Major Pew; the two troops of Bombay Horse Artillery, commanded by Captains Martin and Cotgrave; and Captain Lloyd's battery of Bombay Foot Artillery, all opened upon the citadel and fortress in a manner which shook the enemy, and did such execution as completely to paralyse and to strike terror into them; and his Excellency begs Brigadier Stevenson, the officers, and men of that arm, will accept his thanks for their good service.

The 19th Regiment Bombay Native Infantry, under the command of Lieutenant-Colonel Stalker, having been placed in position to watch any enemy that might appear on the Cabool road, or approach to attack the camp, had an important post assigned to them, although, as it happened, no enemy made an attack upon them.

In sieges and stormings it does not fall to the lot of cavalry to bear the same conspicuous part as to the other two arms of the profession. On this occasion, Sir John Keane is happy to have an opportunity of thanking Major-General Thackwell, and the officers and men of the cavalry divisions under his orders, for having successfully executed the directions given, to sweep the plain, and to intercept fugitives of the enemy attempting to escape from the fort in any direction around it; and had an enemy appeared for the relief of the place during the storming, his Excellency is fully satisfied that the different regiments of this fine arm would have distinguished themselves, and that the opportunity alone was wanting.

Major-General Willshire's division having been broken up for the day, to be distributed as it was, the Major-General was desired to be in attendance upon the Commander-in-Chief. To him and to the officers of the Assistant Quartermaster-General's department of the Bengal and Bombay army, his Excellency returns his warmest thanks for the assistance they have afforded him.

The Commander-in-Chief feels—and in which feeling he is sure he will be joined by the troops composing the Army of the Indus—

that, after the long and harassing marches they have had, and the privations they have endured, this glorious achievement, and the brilliant manner in which the troops have met and conquered their enemy, reward them for it all. His Excellency will only add, that no army that has ever been engaged in a campaign deserves more credit than that which he has the honour to command, for patient, orderly, and correct conduct, under all circumstances, and Sir John Keane is proud to have the opportunity of thus publicly acknowledging it.

By order of his Excellency Lieutenant-General Sir John Keane, Commander-in-Chief of the Army of the Indus.

(Signed) R. Macdonald, Lieut.-Colonel,
Military Secretary, and Deputy Adjutant-Gen. of her Majesty's Forces, Bombay.

ENTRANCE INTO CABOOL.

(*From the Delhi Gazette Extraordinary, of Thursday, Aug.* 29.)

NOTIFICATION.—SECRET DEPARTMENT.

Simla, August 26th, 1839.

The Governor-General of India publishes for general information, the subjoined copy and extracts of despatches from his Excellency the Commander-in-Chief of the Army of the Indus, and from the Envoy and Minister at the Court of his Majesty Shah Shooja-ool-Moolk, announcing the triumphant entry of the Shah into Cabool, on the 7th instant.

In issuing this notification, the Governor-General cannot omit the opportunity of offering to the officers and men composing the army of the Indus, and to the distinguished leader by whom they have been commanded, the cordial congratulations of the government upon the happy result of a campaign, which, on the sole occasion when resistance was opposed to them, has been gloriously marked by victory, and in all the many difficulties of which the character of a British army for gallantry, good conduct, and discipline has been nobly maintained.

A salute of twenty-one guns will be fired on the receipt of this intelligence at all the principal stations of the army in the three Presidencies.

By order of the Right Hon. the Governor-General of India,

T. H. Maddock,
Officiating Secretary to the Government of India, with the Governor-General.

(Copy.)

TO THE RIGHT HON. LORD AUCKLAND, G.C.B., ETC.

My Lord,—We have the honour to acquaint your Lordship that the army marched from Ghuzni, *en route* to Cabool, in two columns, on the 30th and 31st ult., his Majesty Shah Shooja-ool-Moolk, with his own troops, forming part of the second column.

On the arrival of the Commander-in-Chief with the first column, at Hyde Khail, on the 1st inst., information reached him, and the same reached the Envoy and Minister at Huft Assaya, that Dost Mahomed, with his army and artillery, were advancing from Cabool, and would probably take up a position at Urghundee or Midan, (the former twenty-four, the latter thirty-six miles from Cabool.) Upon this it was arranged that his Majesty, with the second column, under Major-General Willshire, should join the first column here, and advance together to attack Dost Mahomed, whose son, Mahomed Akhbar, had been recalled from Jellahabad, with the troops guarding the Khyber Pass, and had formed a junction with his father; their joint forces, according to our information, amounting to about 13,000 men.

Every arrangement was made for the King and the army marching in a body from here to-morrow; but in the course of the night, messengers arrived, and since (this morning) a great many chiefs and their followers, announcing the dissolution of Dost Mahomed's army, by the refusal of a great part to advance against us with him, and that he had in consequence fled, with a party of 300 horsemen, in the direction of Bamian, leaving his guns behind him, in position, as they were placed at Urghundee.

His Majesty Shah Shooja has sent forward a confidential officer, with whom has been associated Major Cureton, of her Majesty's 16th Lancers, taking with him a party of 200 men and an officer of artillery, to proceed direct to take possession of those guns, and afterwards such other guns and public stores as may be found in Cabool and the Balla Hissar, in the name of, and for his Majesty Shah Shooja-ool-Moolk, and the King's order will be carried by his own officer with this party, for preserving the tranquillity of the city of Cabool.

A strong party has been detached in pursuit of Dost Mahomed, under some of our most active officers. We continue our march upon Cabool to-morrow, and will reach it on the third day.

We have, &c.,

(Signed) JOHN KEANE, Lieut.-General,
Commander-in-Chief.

(Signed) W. H. MACNAGHTEN,
Envoy and Minister.

Extract from a Letter from his Excellency Lieutenant-General Sir John Keane, K.C.B. and G.C.H., dated Head-Quarters, Camp, Cabool, August 8th, 1839:—

"It gives me infinite pleasure to be able to address my despatch to your Lordship from this capital, the vicinity of which his Majesty Shah Shooja-ool-Moolk and the army under my command reached the day before yesterday. The King entered his capital yesterday afternoon, accompanied by the British Envoy and Minister and the gentlemen of the mission, and by myself, the general and staff officers of this army, and escorted by a squadron of her Majesty's 4th Light Dragoons, and one of her Majesty's 16th Lancers, with Captain Martin's troop of Horse Artillery. His Majesty had expressed a wish that British troops should be present on the occasion, and a very small party only of his own Hindostanee and Afghan troops. After the animating scene of traversing the streets, and reaching the palace in the Bala Hissar, a royal salute was fired, and an additional salvo in the Afghan style, from small guns, resembling wall-pieces, named gingalls, and carried on camels. We heartily congratulated his Majesty on being in possession of the throne and kingdom of his ancestors, and upon the overthrow of his enemies; and after taking leave of his Majesty, we returned to our camp.

"I trust we have thus accomplished all the objects which your Lordship had in contemplation when you planned and formed the army of the Indus, and the expedition into Afghanistan.

"The conduct of the army, both European and native, which your Lordship did me the honour to place under my orders, has been admirable throughout, and, notwithstanding the severe marching and privations they have gone through, their appearance and discipline have suffered nothing, and the opportunity afforded them at Ghuzni of meeting and conquering their enemy has added greatly to their good spirits.

"The joint despatch addressed by Mr Macnaghten and myself to your Lordship, on the 3rd instant, from Shikarbad, will have informed you that at the moment we had made every preparation to attack (on the following day) Dost Mahomed Khan, in his position at Urghundee, where, after his son, Mahomed Akhbar, had joined him from Jellahabad, he had an army amounting to 13,000 men, well armed and appointed, and thirty pieces of artillery, we suddenly learned that he abandoned them all, and fled, with a party of horsemen, on the road to Bamian, leaving his guns in position, as he had placed them to receive our attack.

"It appears that a great part of his army, which was hourly becoming disorganized, refused to stand by him in the position to receive our attack, and that it soon became in a state of dissolution. The great bulk immediately came over to Shah Shooja, tendering their allegiance, and I believe his Majesty will take most of them into his pay.

" It seems that the news of the quick and determined manner in which we took their stronghold, Ghuzni, had such an effect upon the population of Cabool, and perhaps also upon the enemy's army, that Dost Mahomed from that moment began to lose hope of retaining his rule, for even a short time longer, and sent off his family and valuable property towards Bamian ; but marched out of Cabool, with his army and artillery, keeping a bold front towards us until the evening of the 2nd, when all his hopes were at an end by a division in his own camp, and one part of his army abandoning him. So precipitate was his flight, that he left in position his guns, with their ammunition and wagons, and the greater part of the cattle by which they were drawn. Major Cureton, of her Majesty's 16th Lancers, with his party of 200 men, pushed forward, on the 3rd, and took possession of those guns, &c. There were twenty-three brass guns in position, and loaded ; two more at a little distance, which they attempted to take away ; and since then, three more abandoned, still further off on the Bamian road ; thus leaving in our possession twenty-eight pieces of cannon, with all the materiel belonging to them, which are now handed over to Shah Shooja-ool-Moolk."

Extract from a Letter from W. H. Macnaghten, Esq., Envoy and Minister to the Court of Shah Shooja-ool-Moolk, dated Cabool, 9th of August, 1839 :—

" By a letter signed jointly by his Excellency Lieutenant-General Sir John Keane and myself, dated the 3rd inst., the Right Hon. the Governor-General was apprised of the flight of Dost Mahomed Khan.

" The ex-chief was not accompanied by any person of consequence, and his followers are said to have been reduced to below the number of 100 on the day of his departure. In the progress of Shah Shooja-ool-Moolk towards Cabool, his Majesty was joined by every person of rank and influence in the country, and he made his triumphal entry into the city on the evening of the 7th instant. His Majesty has taken up his residence in the Bala Hissar, where he has required the British mission to remain for the present."

(*From the Bombay Government Gazette Extraordinary of August 29th.*)

Simla, August 26th, 1839.

A letter from Shikarbad, of August 3rd, states—

" The chiefs with their military followers are flocking in by thousands. No better commentary on the feeling regarding Dost Mahomed Khan could be given than the fact of his having been able to induce only 300 out of 12,000 men to accompany him ; Capt. Outram and seven other officers accompany the pursuing party."

The dates from the army at Cabool are to August the 9th. The letters from thence give the following intelligence :—

" The Shah's reception at this place was equally gratifying as at Candahar, though the enthusiasm was not so boisterous.

" We arrived here yesterday, and, I am happy to say, with a sufficient stock of supplies in our Godown to render us quite independent of any foreign purchases for the next ten days, which will keep down prices, and save us from the extravagant rates which we were obliged to purchase at when we reached Candahar. I have not been to the city yet, but am told it is far superior to Candahar. Our people are now very well off; for the increased rations, and abundance and cheapness of grain as we came along, have left them nothing to want or wish for."

Extract of a further letter from Shikarbad, August 3rd :—

" The Afghans have not yet recovered from their astonishment at the rapidity with which Ghuzni fell into our hands, nor up to this moment will they believe how it was effected.

"This morning we received intelligence of Dost Mahomed's flight towards Bamian; for several days past many of his former adherents had been joining the King. Since this morning, thousands of Afghans have been coming in to tender their allegiance to his Majesty, who is in the greatest spirits at this pacific termination to the campaign, and says that God has now granted all his wishes,—Cabool is at hand!

"We are all delighted at it. Few armies have made so long a march in the same time that the army of the Indus has done. The country is every day improving. The road to Candahar from where we are now encamped lies in a continued valley seldom stretching in width above two miles; cultivation on each side of the road, and numberless villages nestling under the hills. Since we left Ghuzni, the fruits have assumed a very fine appearance; the grapes, plums, and apples have become very large, like their brethren of Europe. The climate now is very fine. The rapid Loghurd river is flowing close to our encampments, and the European soldiers and officers are amusing themselves with fishing in it. We are beginning to get vegetables again. I passed this morning through fields of beans, but only in flower. Our attention must be turned to the cultivation of potatoes; they grow in quantities in Persia, and this seems to be just the country for them. To revert from small things to great: a party has just been detached towards Bamian with the view of cutting off Dost Mahomed. It would be a great thing to catch him. The party consists chiefly of Afghans, headed by Hajee Khan Kaukur, and about eight or ten British officers have been sent with it, to prevent the Afghans from committing excesses."

FROM THE

LONDON GAZETTE EXTRAORDINARY,

Thursday, Feb. 13th.

INDIA BOARD, FEB. 13TH.

A DESPATCH has been this day received at the East India House, addressed by the Governor-General of India to the Secret Committee of the East India Company, of which the following is a copy:—

"Camp at Bhurtpore, Dec. 12th, 1839.

"I do myself the honour to forward copies of the despatches noted in the margin, relative to the assault and capture of the fort of Kelat.

"2. The decision, the great military skill, and excellent dispositions of Major-General Willshire, in conducting the operations against Kelat, appear to me deserving the highest commendation. The gallantry, steadiness, and soldier-like bearing of the troops under his command rendered his plans of action completely successful; thereby again crowning our arms across the Indus with signal victory.

"3. I need not expatiate on the importance of this achievement, from which the best effects must be derived, not only in the vindication of our national honour, but also in confirming the security of intercourse between Sinde and Afghanistan, and in promoting the safety and tranquillity of the restored monarchy; but I would not omit to point out that the conduct on this occasion of Major-General Willshire, and of the officers and men under his command, (including the 31st regiment of Bengal Native Infantry, which had not been employed in the previous active operations of the campaign,) have entitled them to more prominent notice that I was able to give them in my general order of November 18th; and in recommending these valuable services to the applause of the committee, I trust that I shall not be considered as going beyond my proper province in stating an earnest hope that the conduct of Major-General Willshire in the direction of the operations will not fail to elicit the approbation of her Majesty's Government.—I have, &c.

"AUCKLAND."

GENERAL ORDERS,

By the Governor-General of India.

Camp Doothanee, December 4th, 1839.

The many outrages and murders committed, in attacks on the followers of the army of the Indus, by the plundering tribes in the neighbourhood of the Bolan Pass, at the instigation of their chief, Meer Mehrab Khan, of Kelat, at a time when he was professing friendship for the British Government, and negotiating a treaty with its representatives, having compelled the government to direct a detachment of the army to proceed to Kelat for the exaction of retribution from that chieftain, and for the execution of such arrangements as would establish future security in that quarter, a force, under the orders of Major-General Willshire, C.B., was employed on this service; and the Right Hon. the Governor-General of India having this day received that officer's report of the successful accomplishment of the objects intrusted to him, has been pleased to direct that the following copy of his despatch, dated the 14th ultimo, be published for general information.

The Governor-General is happy to avail himself of this opportunity to record his high admiration of the signal gallantry and spirit of the troops engaged on this occasion, and offers, on the part of the government, his best thanks to Major-General Willshire, and to the officers and men who served under him.

By command of the Governor-General,

T. H. MADDOCK,

Officiating Secretary to the Government of India, with the Governor-General.

FROM MAJOR-GENERAL SIR THOMAS WILLSHIRE, K.C.B., TO THE GOVERNOR-GENERAL OF INDIA.

Camp, near Kelat, Nov. 14th, 1839.

My Lord,—In obedience to the joint instructions furnished to me by his Excellency the Commander-in-Chief of the Army of the Indus, and the Envoy and Minister to his Majesty Shah Shooja, under date Cabool, the 17th of September, 1839, deputing to me the duty of deposing Mehrab Khan of Kelat, in consequence of the avowed hostility of that chief to the British nation during the present campaign, I have the honour to report, that on my arrival at Quettah, on the 31st ultimo, I communicated with Captain Bean, the political agent in Shawl, and arranged with him the best means of giving effect to the orders I had received.

In consequence of the want of public carriage, and the limited quantity of commissariat supplies at Quettah, as well as the reported want of forage on the route to Kelat, I was obliged to despatch to Cutch Gundava the whole of the cavalry and the greater portion of the artillery, taking with me only the troops noted in the margin,* and leaving Quettah on the 3rd instant.

During the march, the communications received from Mehrab Khan were, so far from acceding to the terms offered, that he threatened resistance if the troops approached his capital. I therefore proceeded, and arrived at the village of Giranee, within eight miles of Kelat, on the 12th instant.

Marching thence the following morning, a body of horse were perceived on the right of the road, which commenced firing on the advanced guard, commanded by Major Pennycuick, her Majesty's 17th regiment, as the column advanced, and the skirmishing between them continued until we came in sight of Kelat, rather less than a mile distant.

* Two guns Bombay Horse Artillery; four guns Shah's ditto; two Ressalaghs Local Horse; Queen's Royals; Her Majesty's 17th regiment; 31st regiment Bengal Native Infantry; Bombay Engineers.

I now discovered that three heights on the north-west face of the fort, and parallel to the north, were covered with infantry, with five guns in position, protected by small parapet walls.

Captain Peat, chief engineer, immediately reconnoitered; and having reported that nothing could be done until those heights were in our possession, I decided upon at once storming them simultaneously, and, if practicable, entering the fort with the fugitives, as the gate in the northern face was occasionally opened to keep up the communication between the fort and the heights.

To effect this object I detached a company from each of the European regiments from the advanced guard with Major Pennycuick, her Majesty's 17th regiment, for the purpose of occupying the gardens and enclosures to the north-east of the town, and two more companies in the plain, midway between them and the column; at the same time I ordered three columns of attack to be formed, composed of four companies from each corps, under their respective commanding officers, Major Carruthers, of the Queen's, Lieutenant-Colonel Croker, her Majesty's 17th regiment, and Major Western, 31st Bengal Native Infantry, the whole under the command of Brigadier Baumgardt, the remainder of the regiments forming three columns of reserve, under my own direction, to move in support.

A hill being allotted to each column, Brigadier Stevenson, commanding the artillery, moved quickly forward in front towards the base of the heights, and when within the required range opened fire upon the infantry and guns, under cover of which the columns moved steadily on, and commenced the ascent for the purpose of carrying the heights, exposed to the fire of the enemy's guns, which had commenced while the columns of attack were forming.

Before the columns reached their respective summits of the hills, the enemy, overpowered by the superior and well-directed fire of our artillery, had abandoned them, attempting to carry off their guns, but which they were unable to do. At this moment, it appearing to me the opportunity offered for the troops to get in with the fugitives, and if possible gain possession of the gate of the fortress, I despatched orders to the Queen's Royal and 17th Regiments to make a rush from the heights for that purpose, following myself to the summit of the nearest, to observe the result. At this moment, the four companies on my left, which had been detached to the gardens and plain, seeing the chance that offered of entering the fort, moved rapidly forward from their respective points towards the gateway, under a heavy and well-directed fire from the walls of the fort and citadel, which were thronged by the enemy.

The gate having been closed before the troops moving towards it could effect the desired object, and the garrison strengthened by the enemy driven from the heights, they were compelled to cover themselves, as far as practicable, behind some walls and ruined buildings to the right and left of it, while Brigadier Stevenson, having ascended the heights with the artillery, opened two guns, under the command of Lieutenant Foster, Bombay Horse Artillery, upon the defences above the gate and its vicinity, while the fire of two others, commanded by Lieutenant Cowper, Shah's Artillery, was directed against the gate itself; the remaining two, with Lieutenant Creed, being sent round to the road on the left hand, leading directly up to the gate, and when within two hundred yards, commenced fire, for the purpose of completing in blowing it open, and after a few rounds, they succeeded in knocking in one half of it. On observing this, I rode down the hill towards the gate, pointing to it, thereby announcing to the troops it was open. They instantly rose from their cover and rushed in. Those under the command of Major Pennycuick, being the nearest, were the first to gain the gate, headed by that officer, the whole of the storming columns from the three regiments rapidly following and gaining an entrance, as quick as it was possible to do so, under a heavy fire from the works and from the interior, the enemy making a most gallant and determined resistance, disputing every inch of ground up to the walls of the inner citadel.

At this time I directed the reserve column to be brought near the gate, and detached one company of the 17th Regiment, under Captain Darley, to the western side of the fort, followed by a portion of the 31st Bengal Native Infantry, commanded by Major Western, conducted by Captain Outram, acting as my extra Aide-de-Camp, for the purpose of securing the heights, under which the southern angle is situated, and intercepting any of the garrison escaping from that side; having driven off the enemy from the heights above, the united detachments then descended to the gate of the fort below, and forced it open before the garrison (who closed it as they saw the troops approach) had time to secure it.

When the party was detached by the western face, I also sent two companies from the reserve of the 17th, under Major Deshon, and two guns of the Shah's artillery, under the command of Lieutenant Creed, Bombay Artillery, by the eastern to the southern face, for the purpose of blowing open the gate above alluded to, had it been necessary, as well as the gate of the inner citadel; the infantry joining the other detachments, making their way through the town in the direction of the citadel.

After some delay, the troops that held possession of the town at length succeeded in forcing an entrance into the citadel, where a desperate resistance was made by Mehrab Khan, at the head of his people; he himself, with many of his principal chiefs, being killed sword in hand. Several others, however, kept up a fire upon our troops from detached buildings difficult of access, and it was not until late in the afternoon, that those that survived were induced to give themselves up on a promise of their lives being spared.

From every account, I have reason to believe the garrison consisted of upwards of 2000 fighting men, and that the son of Mehrab Khan had been expected to join him from Nerosky, with a further reinforcement; the enclosed return will shew the strength of the force under my command present at the capture.

The defences of the fort, as in the case of Ghuzni, far exceeded in strength what I had been led to suppose from previous report, and the towering height of the inner citadel was most formidable, both in appearance and reality.

I lament to say that the loss of killed and wounded on our side has been severe, as will be seen by the accompanying return; that on the part of the enemy must have been great, but the exact number I have not been able to ascertain. Several hundreds of prisoners were taken, from whom the political agent has selected those he considers it necessary for the present to retain in confinement; the remainder have been liberated.

It is quite impossible for me sufficiently to express my admiration of the gallant and steady conduct of the officers and men upon this occasion; but the fact of less than an hour having elapsed from the formation of the columns for the attack to the period of the troops being within the fort, and this performed in the open day, and in the face of an enemy so very superior in numbers, and so perfectly prepared for resistance, will, I trust, convince your Lordship how deserving the officers and troops are of my warmest thanks, and of the highest praise that can be bestowed.

To Brigadier Baumgardt, commanding the storming column, my best thanks are due, and he reports that Captain Willie, acting Assistant Adjutant-General, and Captain Gilland, his aide-de-camp, ably assisted him, and zealously performed their duties; also to Brigadier Stevenson, commanding the artillery, and Lieutenants Forster and Cowper, respectively in charge of the Bombay and Shah's artillery. I feel greatly indebted for the steady and scientific manner in which the service of dislodging the enemy from the heights, and afterwards effecting an entrance into the fort, was performed. The Brigadier has brought to my notice the assistance he received from Captain Coghlan, his brigade-major, Lieutenant Woosnam, his aide-de-camp, and Lieutenant Creed, when in battery yesterday.

To Lieutenant-Colonel Croker, commanding her Majesty's 17th Regiment; Major Carruthers, commanding the Queen's Royals; Major Western, commanding the Bengal 31st Native Infantry, I feel highly indebted for the manner in which they conducted their respective columns to the attack of the heights, and afterwards to the assault of the town, as well as to Major Pennycuick, of the 17th, who led the advance-guard companies to the same point.

To Captain Peat, chief engineer, and to the officers and men of the Engineer Corps, my acknowledgments are due; to Major Neil

Campbell, Acting Quartermaster-General of the Bombay army; to Captain Hagart, Acting Deputy Adjutant-General; and to Lieutenant Ramsay, acting Assistant Quartermaster-General, my best thanks are due for the able assistance afforded me by their services.

From my Aides-de-camp, Captain Robinson and Lieutenant Halket, as well as from Captain Outram, who volunteered his services on my personal staff, I received the utmost assistance; and to the latter officer I feel greatly indebted for the zeal and ability with which he has performed various duties that I have required of him, upon other occasions, as well as the present.

It is with much pleasure that I state the great assistance I have received from Captain Bean in obtaining supplies.

T. WILLSHIRE,
Major-Gen., Commanding Bombay Column,
Army of the Indus.

Return of Casualties in the army under the command of Major-General Willshire, C.B., employed at the storming of Kelat, on the 13*th of November,* 1839:—

1st Troop of Cabool Artillery—2 rank and file, 6 horses, wounded.

Gun Lancers attached to ditto—1 rank and file, 1 horse, wounded; 1 corporal, since dead.

Her Majesty's 2nd, or Queen's Royal Regiment—1 lieutenant, 21 rank and file, killed; 2 captains, 2 lieutenants, 1 adjutant, 2 sergeants, 40 rank and file, 1 horse, wounded.

Her Majesty's 17th Regiment—6 rank and file, killed; 1 captain, 3 sergeants, 29 rank and file, wounded.

31st Regiment of Bengal Native Infantry—1 subadar, 2 rank and file, killed; 1 captain, 1 ensign, 2 jemadars, 2 sergeants, 1 drummer, 14 rank and file, 1 bheestie, wounded.

Sappers and Miners and Pioneers—1 sergeant wounded.

4th Bengal Local Horse—1 rank and file wounded.

Total—1 lieutenant, 1 subadar, 29 rank and file, killed; 4 captains, 2 lieutenants, 1 ensign, 1 adjutant, 2 jemadars, 8 sergeants, 1 drummer, 87 rank and file, 1 bheestie, 7 horses, wounded.

Total killed and wounded—138.

Names of Officers killed and wounded.

Killed—Her Majesty's 2nd or Queen's Royal Regiment—Lieutenant T. Gravatt.

Wounded—Her Majesty's 2nd, or Queen's Royal Regiment—Captain W. M. Lyster, Captain T. Sealy, Lieutenant T. W. E. Holdsworth, severely; Lieutenant D. J. Dickenson, slightly; Adjutant J. E. Simmons, severely.

Her Majesty's 17th Regiment—Captain L. C. Bourchier, severely.

31st Regiment of Bengal Native Infantry—Captain Saurin, slightly; Ensign Hopper, severely.

C. HAGART, Captain,
Acting Deputy Adjutant-Gen. Bombay Column, Army of the Indus.

State of the Corps engaged at the storming of Kelat, on the 13*th of November,* 1839, *under the command of Major-General Willshire, C.B.*

Camp at Kelat, November 13th, 1839.

Staff—1 major-general, 2 brigadiers, 5 aides-de-camp, 1 acting deputy-adjutant-general, 1 acting quartermaster-general, 1 deputy assistant-quartermaster-general, 2 brigade-majors, 1 sub-assistant commissary-general.

Detachment 3rd Troop Horse Artillery—2 lieutenants, 2 sergeants, 36 rank and file.

1st Troop Cabool Artillery—1 lieutenant, 8 sergeants, 1 drummer, 1 farrier, 58 rank and file.

Her Majesty's 2nd, or Queen's Royal Regiment—1 major, 3 captains, 7 lieutenants, 1 ensign, 1 adjutant, 31 serjeants, 10 drummers, 290 rank and file.

Her Majesty's 17th Regiment—1 lieutenant-colonel, 2 majors, 4 captains, 13 lieutenants, 2 ensigns, 1 quartermaster, 1 surgeon, 29 sergeants, 9 drummers, 338 rank and file.

31st Regiment Bengal Native Infantry—1 major, 2 captains, 3 lieutenants, 2 ensigns, 1 adjutant, 1 quartermaster, 1 surgeon, 12 native officers, 30 sergeants, 14 drummers, 329 rank and file.

Sappers and Miners and Pioneers—1 captain, 1 lieutenant, 1 assistant surgeon, 3 native officers, 1 sub-conductor, 7 sergeants, 3 drummers, 117 rank and file.

Total—1 major-general, 2 brigadiers, 5 aides-de-camp, 1 acting deputy adjutant-general, 1 acting quartermaster-general, 1 deputy assistant-quartermaster-general, 2 brigade-majors, 1 sub-assistant-commissary-general, 1 lieutenant-colonel, 4 majors, 10 captains, 27 lieutenants, 5 ensigns, 2 adjutants, 2 quartermasters, 2 surgeons, 1 assistant-surgeon, 15 native officers, 1 sub-conductor, 107 sergeants, 37 drummers, 1 farrier, 1,166 rank and file.

The Sappers and Miners and Pioneers were not engaged until the gate was taken.

C. Hagart, Captain,
Acting Deputy Adjutant-Gen., Bombay Column, Army of the Indus.

Note—Two russalas of the Bengal Local Horse remained in charge of the baggage during the attack.

List of Beloochee Sirdars killed in the assault of Kelat, on the 13th of November, 1839 :—

Meer Mehrab Khan, Chief of Kelat.

Meer Wullee Mahomed, the Muengul Sirdar of Wudd.

Abdool Kurreem, Ruhsanee Sirdar.

Dad Kurreen, Shahwanee Sirdar.

Mahomed Ruzza, nephew of the Vizier Mahomed Hoosein.

Khysur Khan, Ahsehrie Sirdar.

Dewan Bucha Mull, Financial Minister.

Noor Mahomed and Taj Mahomed, Shagassa Sirdars.

Prisoners.

Mahomed Hoossein, Vizier.

Moola Ruheem Dad, ex-Naib of Shawl; with several others of inferior rank.

J. D. D. DEAN, Political Agent.

CAPTURE OF THE FORT AND CITADEL OF KELAT.

Political Department, Fort William, Dec. 14, 1839.

The Hon. the President in Council has much satisfaction in publishing the following despatch from Major-General Willshire, C.B., with the returns annexed to it, reporting the capture of the fort and citadel of Kelat, by storm, on the 13th of November, which brilliant achievement was effected by a force consisting of only 1200 men, with the loss, his Honour in Council grieves to say, of 138 killed and wounded, including amongst the former one officer, Lieutenant Gravatt, of her Majesty's 2nd, or Queen's Regiment, and amongst the latter, eight officers.

Meer Mehrab Khan himself, and eight other sirdars, were amongst the slain of the enemy.

The general order issued by the Right Hon. the Governor-General, on the receipt of this intelligence, is republished, and his Honour in Council unites with his Lordship in recording his high admiration of the signal gallantry and spirit of the troops engaged, and in offering his thanks to Major-General Willshire, and to the officers and men who served under him on this occasion.

A royal salute will be fired from the ramparts of Fort William, at noon this day, in honour of the event.

By order of the Hon. the President in Council,

H. T. PRINSEP,

Secretary to the Government of India.